Ringing Here & There
A NATURE CALENDAR

Also by Brian Bartlett

Poetry

Potato Blossom Road: Seven Montages
Being Charlie
The Watchmaker's Table
Travels of the Watch
Wanting the Day: Selected Poems
The Afterlife of Trees
Granite Erratics
Underwater Carpentry
Planet Harbor
Cattail Week

Edited

The Essential Robert Gibbs
The Essential James Reaney
Earthly Pages: The Poetry of Don Domanski
Don McKay: Essays on His Works

Ringing Here & There
A NATURE CALENDAR

BRIAN BARTLETT

Fitzhenry & Whiteside

Published in Canada by Fitzhenry & Whiteside
195 Allstate Parkway, Markham
ON, L3R 4T8
www.fitzhenry.ca

Published in the U.S. by Fitzhenry & Whiteside
311 Washington Street, Brighton,
Massachusetts 02135

Edited by Evan Jones
Cover image courtesy Donald R. Pentz (Studio 21)
Cover painting: Don Pentz, "Enigma Landscape #64"
Text and cover design by Daniel Choi

We acknowledge with thanks the Canada Council for the Arts, and the Ontario Arts Council for their support of our publishing program. We acknowledge the financial support of the Government of Canada through the Canada Book Fund (CBF) for our publishing activities.

Canada Council   Conseil des Arts
for the Arts   du Canada

ONTARIO ARTS COUNCIL
CONSEIL DES ARTS DE L'ONTARIO
50 YEARS OF ONTARIO GOVERNMENT SUPPORT OF THE ARTS
50 ANS DE SOUTIEN DU GOUVERNEMENT DE L'ONTARIO AUX ARTS

Library and Archives Canada Cataloguing in Publication
Bartlett, Brian, 1953-, author
    Ringing here and there : a nature calendar / Brian Bartlett.
Poems.
ISBN 978-1-55455-331-0 (pbk.)
    1. Human ecology--Poetry. I. Title.
PS8553.A773R55 2014   C811'.54   C2014-901002-8

Publisher Cataloging-in-Publication Data (U.S.)
Ringing Here & There: A Nature Calendar
ISBN 978-1-55455-331-0
Data available on file

Printed and bound in Canada

MIX
Paper from
responsible sources
FSC
www.fsc.org
FSC® C016245

CONTENTS

AUTHOR'S NOTE

Out to the icebox to replenish my intuitions. Body drags soul into the changeable. The feeling that one is on the edge of many things. Lord of Laughter & Light, attend me. A thing can be small but it need not be a cameo. The splendid irrationality of a peacock's tail. The self must be a bridge, not a pit. A morning without precedent.

A collage of bits from *Straw for the Fire: From the Notebooks of Theodore Roethke 1943-63.*

The drafting of this book of days began in April 2010 & concluded two years later, in April 2012. Then I picked 366 paragraphs (not forgetting leap years) from over 440 written, & interwove the two years into one. Many paragraphs ended up assigned a day of the year other than the one on which they originated, but usually I kept them within the month of their original creation. Sustained

& linked by their observations of non-human phenomena, these slices of prose were influenced by decades of reading diarists & nature writers (some individuals being one & the same). No writer has taught me more about keeping alert, being tenacious & using words than Thoreau, but a few months after embarking on the project I also recalled my fondness for Donald Culross Peattie's 365-entry, spring-to-spring book of nature writing, *An Almanac for Moderns* (1935). After completing most or all of the work here, I also came across volumes such as *The Folio Book of Days,* edited by Roger Hudson (2002), with its excerpts from many authors; Fred Waage's *Sinking Creek Journal: An Environmental Book of Days* (2010), which goes from one September to the next; Dan Soucoup's historically oriented *The Maritime Book of Days* (1999); Deng Ming-Dao's *365 Tao: Daily Meditations* (1992); Steve Grant's compilation from many years of Thoreau's journals, *Daily Observations: The Days of the Year* (2005); &—a book on my shelves for nearly forty years, yet unread & utterly forgotten through the writing of *Ringing Here & There*—Edwin May Teale's *Circle of the Seasons: The Journal of a Naturalist's* Year (1953).

One 21st-century aspect of *Ringing Here & There* is that its paragraphs were all posted as Facebook "updates." Longer than haiku but shorter than sonnets, the entries shared during the first sixteen months were kept necessarily within the 420-character maximum of Facebook postings. I playfully enjoyed the challenge of the length limit, so when that limit was eliminated by the mysterious Facebook powers-that-be, I stubbornly stuck to a visually accustomed sense of the entries' maximum size, without being confined by a fanatical adherence to 420 or fewer characters. Other than ironically declaring their independence from Facebook by rejecting its change of update lengths, from the beginning the paragraphs had rebelled against many other characteristics of the famous, infamous social-networking forum: they were all first handwritten and revised by pen, usually underwent further revisions after being posted, always included some element of the natural world, were rooted in the paragraph more than the fragment or the sentence, valued the mighty ampersand as a beautifully-shaped concentrator, & subsequently had other lives, such as appearances in literary journals & at public readings or conferences. I began to think of the handwritten drafts as their infancy & childhood; Facebook postings as their adolescence; & later appearances—including in this book—as their maturity. While some of the entries might be called prose poems, I've resisted that as a label for them all, considering other terms such as field reports, sketches, commentaries, tributes, laments, micro-narratives, quotations, & collages.

APRIL

...flashes in its onrushing...

1

Hour of spangled light & forked shadows. Branches & trunks break up late-afternoon sun-rays, so the air is a mix of diamonds, stars & slivers, instigator of blinks & squints. Then I step out of brightness into shadows thrown across the trail like giant splayed claws. Light & shade alternate so dramatically that only at the hour's end do I realize I've not once lifted the binoculars to my eyes.

2

Early evening in the dense shelter & serpentine pathways of Hemlock Ravine. The quiet was an amplifier: a single distant Mourning Dove's voice was hardly filtered by the 300-year-old hemlocks & other trees grappling for the sky. That hollow voice, that oboe lingering over one note—why say it's "mourning"? With snow still laced under surfaced roots, a Wooing Dove.

3

Two black dogs off their leashes lunged along the evening beach, excited, as if in attack mode—but ignored us & sped into further freedom & space. Over the ocean an hour later, sundogs glowed on either side of the horizon-halved sun—light caught in ice fog's crystals, fractured, comet-like, that sun's surrogates or pets. We might've called the evening Concentration, there at a beach named Crystal Crescent.

4

Walked in old sneakers around ancient land outside West Dover, on curvy road to Peggy's Cove: boggy, twiggy, scattered with giant erratics shoved there by glaciers, now dotted & streaked with lichens. Pitcher Plants starting to rise up, crawling junipers inching along rock, bushes far more plentiful than trees, a few coyote scats threaded with hare fur. Everywhere, golds & browns & rusts.

5

In Timberlea, a walk while afternoon meets evening. I think of some species mostly in flocks, swarms, flotillas, so it feels unfamiliar to hear just one Canada Goose honk (once) & one Spring Peeper shrill (once). Catching wind of a single Loon or Raven would be more standard. Soon a trio of geese flap past: good to have our numbers revised, our patterns of thought shaken, broken.

6

The spring's first Grackles are back, their rusty-metal voices scraping as they flutter between spruces. A Blue Jay rips air with attention-seizing shrieks. Even a Starling's mimicry today favours the harsh over the whistled or warbled. It's as if all the gentle-voiced are absent, or resting, reserving their strength, the day made by a blacksmith from whose anvil varied hardnesses ring. A Raven sounds like he agrees.

7

Caught in the lower twigs of a stunted conifer, is that Bear Hair lichen? When I reach the tree & tug one of the two clumps, actual fur comes away in my fingers, as if the two sides of a metaphor changed places, bear hair resembling the lichen named after it. Then I put the discovery to my nose & sniff, & the metaphor falls to the earth like a wizened berry because I recognize *wet dog, wet dog, wet dog.*

8

Awake again, Little Brown Bats emerge during the day, since the nights are still too cold for flies to flick about. The bats tolerate more light now than in June & July. Later they will feast in the darkest hours, when flies seek blood & feces until dawn. But for now, leaning toward summer, spring still presses a reluctant shoulder back against winter, & bats circle a pond under a white sky hinting of sunlight.

9

On a bank where a lake & a brook meet, wood chips are strewn around poplar stumps ringed with teeth marks. Since the lake is so close, the beavers need build no dam, but their lodge was recently patched & freshened. They share the neighbourhood with a species suggested by signs caught among the branches & mud: a bicycle tire, a white plastic bucket, chip bags, a torn t-shirt with a cartoon hawk across its front.

10

With closed eyes name objects by smelling them—ginger, lemon, pears. Observe how far the Big Dipper moves in two hours. Compare the cow's tail to that of the horse, the deer, the goat. Compare the rabbit's mode of washing with the cat's. Draw a frog swimming. If a large hailstone is found, cut it across, then describe the cut face. Examine your hand closely.

A collage of quotations from *Public School Nature-Study*, a 1902 Copp Clark school text.

11

One morning when I was twelve my mother sent me down the street on a strawberry-picking mission to the house of my uncle the beekeeper. Instead I foraged for raspberries, finding few, filling less than a quarter of the pail. When my mistake was revealed, I fell into silence—the clan's young "nature bug" that much a garden greenhorn! For years afterward, the day I'd confused fruit with fruit tasted of ignorance & shame.

12

Around the Halifax War Memorial, Crows tilt in the air, step through dead grass. I face lettered slabs afixed to stone, hundreds of names of the vanished & unburied, all in ranks. Is that a Lance Corporal with leaf in beak, a Nursing Sister with pointed wing, a Yeoman of Signals calling? Steward, Stoker, Electrical Artificer—or, *Corvus brachyrhynchos*, are you all unranked, a level playing-field of glossy black?

13

The night before a birding trip, I dreamed of a giant, borderless field. Red-tailed Hawks crossed the cloudlessness, then eagles, followed by owls larger than any owls in the waking world. And what were those speedy, blackness-wrapped, grotesque-faced ones, those deformed vultures? Oh yes, only Dementors, from the Harry Potter movies—neither fearful nor marvellous since I was hoping for a species utterly unknown.

14

Fast even for sandpipers, six Sanderlings scoot along the tide line at Martinique Beach, their silver & white feathers wind-stroked & morning-lit. Their synchronized darting doesn't blur their legs or lessen their separate selves (each is one of six). What coins can match their living glitter as they patter over pale sand, against a backdrop of dark water? Two hours after sunrise, they are the apotheosis of silver.

15

Ever since storms lifted plateaus of sand & rerouted the water, Bayers Island has worn its name loosely, now part of the mainland, yet easy to tell from the sandy beach. Low tangles of Crowberry thrive, their ruddy needles haphazardly interrupted by green, accentuating the paleness of an Ipswich Sparrow. The island-that-was is a furry red animal stranded next to a giant pale-skinned body sprawling into the distance.

16

Bluff Wilderness Trail. Hike in silently, we dozen agreed, save all talking for the return. An hour later one of us protested, as if afraid her tongue would go numb. The rest of us voted for loyalty to our vow. Silence had been severed, but in the next hour the voices of Golden-crowned Kinglets, Juncos & a Broad-winged Hawk sewed it back together—until at 3:00 p.m. we all pulled it apart again with the claws & beaks of our words.

17

Recent rain has slicked everything at our feet. Black Felt Lichen sticks to granite like bits of burned maps. Thick as body-builders' arms, tree roots muscle over the muddy trail. Through the forest, boulders were scattered by Glooscap's pea-shooter. One lake called Pot, another called Cranberry. Granite & root, root & rock. Talk, & your chances of slipping or tripping multiply.

18

The forest is full of compensations: spruce shade makes a slight chill but keeps the sun from burning us, death nestles in every cranny but Carrion Beetles hide the corpses & are nourished. Facing stripped poplars & birches, I miss the absent leaves' play with light—but on this rocky ridge, through all those openings among the branches, I see the lake more widely than I will in thickly leafed summer.

19

A sign by this forest trail warned me of bears & moose, but I've not even seen a squirrel or a mouse. On an rough-rock opening, a Garter Snake out of hibernation is feasting on an American Toad, hind legs jutting from the stretched mouth, a bulge pulsing. If any signs warning amphibians against reptiles are nearby—YOU ARE ENTERING SNAKE COUNTRY—they're too entangled at ground level, & too fine, for me to read.

20

fertile & dewy intinct. particularly in young specamens. an insame ambition to perpetuate the memory of themselves. those slight labos which afford me a livelihood. the gohst of the ample stream that once flowed to the ocean. all the world reflicted in our depths. late sunmer. the quitness of the hour. I conciliated the gouds by some sacrament as bathing. a few good anecdoes is our science.

A collage of passages including misspellings, from the manuscripts of Thoreau's journals as transcribed in the Princeton University Press editions.

21

On a ridge across the lake, yellow steam-shovels, excavators & bulldozers swivel, thrust & scrape. Half a dozen years ago, my son was thrilled by such machines glimpsed on city streets, & I'd respond by slowing the car down. That time now seems so innocent—yet beloved Greek & British landscapes were prepared centuries ago by ripping out trees. Under the tree-serrated horizon, ancient history continues.

22

As I was crossing a footbridge a Sapsucker zipped past, stung the air with its nasal call, then drummed a few times, only to cry again. Back at the bridge an hour later, an unseen Hermit Thrush launched its ascending rings of fluting tones. The ear was charmed that a scold had given way to music—then the Sapsucker's rasp rang again, & I knew that neither voice was paramount & both belonged to the evening.

23

Rain falls so hard you take off your streaming glasses & walk within the many limits of nearsightedness. A patch of Coltsfoot is a smear of chalked yellow; a Purple Finch, a splurge of strawberry jam. You see like your myopic ancestors before glass was shaped to correct vision. Sharp lines have vanished from this newly alien trail. Your hands grope to pull off the gauze in which the world is wrapped.

24

Driving along Bedford Basin, I listen to Johnny Cash in his dying months, singing in Hendersonville, Tennessee, his voice like a blunted saw: "There ain't no grave can hold my body down." Then I'm in the chilly woods, where a crow with lustreless, troubled feathers lands on a branch above me. His beak moves—nothing but silence comes out. "When I hear that trumpet sound, I'm gonna rise right out of the ground."

25

Owl Survey night: in the Pockwock Watershed woods, we drive for hours of timed stops, play a CD of owl calls from a boom-box on the jeep's hood. Our motionless spells of listening are pools of patience & expectation. Just as I bite into a piece of whiskey-filled toffee to ward off the chill, a Barred Owl lands nearby. Its mix of hoot, bark & babble is even more resonant than the whiskey's warming surprise in my throat.

26

This stream has no name, running underground—maybe for miles—until it breaks from sloped forest & flashes in its onrushing. I'm glad to stand by water that makes music with rocks, foams just a little before it slips into the lake a few paces away, then loses its identity & voice. I'm also glad that streams we know nothing about are hidden, untouchable & unheard, in the darkness far under our feet.

27

6:30 a.m., breakfast on the beach. In the salt marsh, a Great Blue Heron stalks & halts, stalks & halts. A Greater Yellowlegs & a Lesser Yellowlegs—oblivious to each other?—stab the damp sand. Binoculars around my neck, the sound of my teeth biting an apple is sharp. A Red Fox with the thickest fox-tail I've ever seen trots my way, as if expecting the handout of a freshly-killed mouse or a Black Duck's egg.

28

Talk about persistence. For fifteen pre-twilight minutes, from the top of a spruce by Governor's Lake, a silhouetted robin floats many variations onto the air. It's sobering to have lived so long before trying to give the robin's singing its due. The familiar name is American Robin, but nothing especially American about this bird without nationality. & nothing especially colonial-feeling about Governor's Lake.

29

Magpies have two openings into their nest, one to enter into it and one to escape. Colts are running races round the straw yards & rubbing at the gates anxious to greet the sprouting grass & loathing their winter food. Several insects have a shiny quality in the dark, one a "gloworm" by night & the "forty legg'd worm" by day. I have no specimens to send you so be as it may you must be content with my descriptions & observations.

A collage of moments, slightly adapted, from the prose writings of John Clare (1793-1864).

30

I like to think, singularly, "Old Friend Crow, Old Friend Jay, Old Friend Nuthatch"—though that makes the many one, as if each species were just an individual. In childhood I never said that, but now in my sixth decade I do, since I've seen so many of them in so many seasons, years & places. "Old Friend," but this evening the birds on the trail may only be a year or two young, & it's I who am—& was—the oldest.

MAY

...into new configurations...

1

In Hants County, drove past the sign MEANDER RIVER. Love at first sight for the name & the glimpsed flash of water. Imagined being born on the banks of a river named Meander. Later did research: verb "meander" comes from the Buyuk Menderes (Maeander) River in Turkey, first mentioned in Homer's *Iliad*. So in the beginning the river wasn't named after the verb—the verb was named after the river.

2

Turning from the mega-stores of Bayer's Lake Industrial Park, a brief trek into a world of Blueberry & Labrador Tea bushes—then on flat stone openings, three wannabe inuksuit. Towers of rocks whispering, "Disheveled wilderness, bow down." What strangers rolled & lifted the rocks, then gathered sticks to insert as the arms of a man? Those arms have no hands, so they offer no seeds to the winds & the finches.

3

In Hemlock Ravine, the tightly compressed circles & curves of young fern heads, asparagus green or a paler lime, with hints of cinnamon & rust. None of them are the same. Who first said "fiddlehead"? A fiddler improvising a reel or jig while dancers circled each other? It gives hope that such clenched fists open into the tall, wide branchings of full-fledged ferns.

4

On the highway from Halifax to Lunenburg, four dead porcupines. 30,000 quills no defense: *porc-épic* evolution hasn't caught up with cars travelling at contemporary speeds. R.I.P., slow beasts with a taste for birch leaves, old boots, & highway salt. Closer to our destination, a Ring-Necked Pheasant crossed the road, so visible, quick & distant we didn't even need to brake.

5

Flick-floating on brookwater, my first Water Striders of the year step to the left, to the right, their micro-thin legs casting round shadows on the brook's sandy floor. Of course they're not really "my" insects, those water-walkers who need no apparatus to do what they do. A mile away, my daughter stretches, bends, pivots in her Maritime Dance Academy class.

6

Amidst the tapping of fine rain on moss, leaves, twigs & logs, light bells are ringing here & there. A Junco flits up & down branches of a young spruce rooted in a nurse stump: white bordering tail-feathers flick against its grey. What insects stir within the wood rot? Bells interspersed with the subtle rain: those clear voices from all four corners of the compass. Each nurse stump deserves a Junco ringing.

7

Like blue flames fluttering, the first Spring Azures of May on both sides of a boggy trail. They keep their distance. When they alight for half-seconds, their wings fold, the undersides grey, denying their name. One brushes against an empty Labatt's Blue can somebody hooked to a twig. Ahhh-zzzure, ahhhh-zzzzure. I'm left wondering if anything feasts on the pupae that gave birth to those restless bits of blue sky.

8

Overnight, a new colour. After white blossoms—Hawthorne, Serviceberry, Strawberry—rosy-purple Rhodora begin to bloom, sparsely, in these shrubby woods in Timberlea. Five-petalled—the longer two flaring sideways like dancers' legs. What's to be said for these flowers that appear before their leaves? More than we can say. In a week or two, whole bushes will blaze in evening mists, fires that consume nothing.

9

The (my) year's first Green Frog sounds its rubbery, slack pluck, & back in the woods the (my) season's first Flicker speedily goes *wik-wik-wik-wik*. When I bend to re-tie a boot lace, I see the (my) spring's first Purple Trillium, its bloom in suspense between nodding & rising. I've re-focussed *the* into *my*, but *my* too misleads, & the muskrats & perch are concealed, the glimmering marsh too wide to embrace.

10

After a walk in the woods, I drive to Tims for a mug of chai tea & read poetry for half an hour before I realize I've not listened to a moment of the background music—hardly even knew any music played. But in the woods I didn't want to miss any cry, buzz, peep, caw, call or song. Hermit Thrush, Yellow Warbler, welcome back. There my Tims ears would've been a curse, a small deaf pair of plates.

11

Between Ravine Trail & Wentworth Loop, I feel a sharp itch in my throat. I cough. One spring, pollen landed on my eyeball & I ended up in E.R., where they used a needle to freeze my eye & a tiny vacuum to inhale the fluid of an unknown allergy. Is there a single seed floating here that could shut down my lungs? I spit in the ferns. Oh yes, in this forest something far finer than a poisonous mushroom could do me in.

12

By the broader, brighter trails the fiddlehead shapes are gone, replaced by ferns in all their height & breadth. Then you find yourself in a deeper, darker part of the forest, down where sunlight has a hard time reaching, & you come across more clusters of ferns-to-be. In the muck, all these questionmarks with their compact & concentrated heads—this green village still on the edge of transformation.

13

Days on a small island without electricity or running water rope birth & death extra tightly together. Gull chicks an hour old: purple skin, soaked feathers. From their underground burrows, Storm-Petrels staccato-purr through their midnight mating. A dead Minke Whale's stench & its shining bristled baleen. Down on my knees, I cradle in one hand a seal's seawater-washed jawbone with all its teeth intact.

14

Wave after wave of exhausted warblers descend upon the island. A haggard Black-throated Green wanders among beach rocks before re-finding spruce cover. Magnolias with their black necklaces over yellow; thin-voiced Blackpolls; orange-flashing Redstarts & orange-throated Blackburnians: pockets of colour & pockets of song in the grey trees near the hoarse sea. Winds that wet & bit their feathers helped them get this far.

15

Wood Violets—tiny islands of white—make up in numbers what they lack in size, as if spring's first favours went to smallness. In tree tops by the pond Black-crowned Night Herons perch at noon. Washed ashore, shark or tuna line has wound & wound around a driftwood hulk. A Winter Wren sings its high, superlatively speedy song—the days too short & too few for singing everything that should be sung.

16

Six years ago, when Josh was six, on this island I collected owl pellets from under trees, then carried them home, where we fingered the skulls of petrels & voles but didn't dwell on stories of swift death. Now he's with me here on the same island: son & father side-by-side shivering in the chill, gazing into those eyes—yellow eyes with pupils like black holes, those hints of prehistory before any hands gathered bones.

17

Swainson's Thrush, 3. Plastic fuel-oil bottle, 4. Canada Goose, 7. Plastic Coke bottle, 9. Muskrat, 1. Rubber glove, 3 (1 orange, 1 gr, 1 yel). Redstart, 6. Inflatable ball, 5. Boreal Chickadee, 2. White plastic chair, 2. Catbird, 4. Springwater bottle, 5. Northern Harrier, 2. Reference to Deepwater Horizon, calculatingly beautiful name of broken drilling-rig in Gulf of Mexico, 3.

18

This small island is a sponge. The trails are soaked, & the fields, & the quaking earth under dead trees. On this paradise for mosses & lichens, trying to fall asleep, I listen to the woodstove fire making sounds like bugs hitting glass or floor boards sighing, ice melting or salamanders stepping on coals. Shape-changer to our ears, the fire is a bird struggling on the ground in the pitch dark outside the window.

19

Pat has never before brought a cell-phone to the island, but with her daughter's ultra-sound in the offing she did, & now in the clamour of a gull colony an unbirdlike buzz sounds. Pat answers & cries, "A granddaughter!" We cheer. An hour later in a domain of hanging lichen, high up in a nest all broken branches & sharp angles, a pair of Great Horned Owls gaze down at us, a shut-eyed owlet in between.

20

Nothing else all morning moved like the flexible Garter Snake that slid from an abandoned lobster-trap, formed two semi-circles over grass, straightened upon rock, tongue-touched the air, then kinked into new configurations—while far overhead a jet traced a white trail straight as the simplest route from A to Z, the sort of route we spurned during those island days.

21

When I sank my boots in muck rather than choosing a dry patch, the others said, "Not very Left-Brain, are you?" When I saw a samurai warrior in the flames of the camp-fire, Josh laughed, "Oh Dad, you're so Right-Brain!" But when I was trying to sleep, I thought back to the strings & ropes of purple, yellow & green seaweed draped around rocks: all those brains slopping left & right, arranged by the tides' whims.

22

Sometimes I'm awkward as a crow on an icy rock, with a brain soft as walking on eel grass—but there I felt healthy as a trout. One morning we slogged through a dungeon of fog, & shithawks shrieked as we wended our way among their nests, but next day the fogeater was out in all its yellow glory. Sweet Humpbacked Jesus! Everyone needs a pool of still water. May that island persist till the last blue smoke.

> The above paragraph uses nine expressions from Lewis Poteet's *The South Shore Phrase Book*. I found a tattered copy of it in the bunkhouse on Bon Portage Island.

23

While a sleek white cat lounges on the railing of a third-floor balcony, a Blue Jay cries in a tree. The jay hops from branch to branch, throwing volleys of jagged-edged sounds at the cat, who slowly lengthens her ears. Is the jay outraged the cat is higher in the air? Is he feeling *No creature should be so white*? He keeps fidgetting & shrieking. She keeps tightening her muscles, straightening her back.

24

Now dandelions rule the edges of the Rails to Trails path. My daughter rubs the yellow dust along my arm, chanting, "Mommy walked down the aisle—Daddy walked down the aisle—Baby peed down the aisle." Coltsfoot, equally yellow, tough enough to sprout up through gravel, have already shrunken & closed, their year over—the price of being a harbinger.

25

I was born in the breezes. I ran out of potatoes in mid-ocean, & was wretched. To find one's way to lands already discovered is a good thing. My memory worked with the ominous, the insignificant, the great, the small. Old turtles poked their heads up out of the sea as I sang, but the porpoises were more appreciative; one day when I was humming "Babylon's a-Falling," a porpoise jumped higher than the bowsprit.

A scattering of sentences from *Sailing Alone Around the World*, Joshua Slocum's book about his solo circumnavigation of Earth between 1895 and 1898.

26

At an Upper Falmouth farmhouse, the McGowan Lake fish hatchery & Middleton High School, Chimney Swifts gather around roofs & slip into chimneys. At the Robie Tufts Nature Centre in Wolfville & Temperance Street School in New Glasgow, birders' necks stretch & their tabulating eyes flick. Like swifts flecked across the sky at dusk, reports of swifts—& of their counters—stream in along electrical & digital currents.

27

Paint-happy stranger, driving down the highway I see again the colossal red heart you emblazoned on cliffs, with black letters reading GOD GAVE YOUR HEART TO ME. Right, I know you're not addressing me, & I won't begin theological head-butting (who can say what God gave to whom, etc.?)—but would you please, please not spray-paint the land with valentines no rains will wash away?

28

For months the children kept watch over the salmon eggs, then the fingerlings, in the classroom tank. Today my mistake was trusting a kid to map-read, so we got miles off course & missed the release, but the girls roared up the radio, sang, laughed—didn't mind. I was the bereft one, failing to witness the salmon sliding into the river, finned quintessences freed from the tank, instantly at home in their fluent element.

29

Over time beaches rise & sink, advance & withdraw. Grasses come & go, storms relocate bands of rocks, sand shifts around like nomads re-pitching their tents. We've praised trilliums for blooming, butterflies for breaking from a chrysalis—but a beach's mutations are slower, trickier to focus on, so harder to praise. Beaches have more faces than the Harbour Seals, the Savannah Sparrows & we ourselves will ever know.

30

Today when I took our cat to the vet, the cage's rusted door fell off. Rust eats a hole in the wheelbarrow. Rust invades the backyard shed & discolours a rake. Rust weakens the spikes in the backboard of the abandoned basketball net. The shed's doorlatch, the propane tank, the croquet wickets—rusted. Once I found a lost watch in a park: in this oceanside realm of oxides, rust was gnawing on the hands of time.

31

*Give me the man who will go rambling over his own country &
clamber over its rocks, who will dip his digits in its streams & tear
his breeches with its brambles & break the head of any man who at-
tempts to affirm there ever was, or will be, such another Country.* Old
Joe Howe, your pride is feisty, & Nova Scotia runs through my veins
too—but provincial splendours are only a fraction in the mathe-
matics of Earth.

The quotation above is from *Western and Eastern Rambles: Travel Sketches
in Nova Scotia* by Joseph Howe, published originally in *The Novascotian*
from 1828 to 1831.

JUNE

...Black Earthtongue, Goldgill Navelcap...

1

No towns along the way, just one far-horizoned Saskatchewan field after another. We drive into & out of light showers, dark downpours, wind-whipped spittings. Accustomed to Atlantic rains that encompass ten or twelve counties, I've never before been caught up in such a sequence of local rainfalls. A long-legged rabbit—like a sleek sea-creature fathoms deep—bounds off the pavement, into wavering grasses.

2

On my father-in-law's ancestral farm an hour north of Calgary, the beavers disappeared after downing all the alders by the creek. In retirement, Ralph then planted spruces ("beavers won't touch them"), but badgers mistook the broken soil for gophers' work & uprooted the trees. Ralph placed slabs of rock at the tree bases &— he's unsure why—the seedlings are now undisturbed, as if rock were a peace-maker between badger & man.

3

Beyond my feet, Fish Creek is wider than some rivers. On its other side a forest rises, steep, nearly perpendicular. I'm eating a sandwich, resting with legs over the bank, wondering why those White Spruces shed their cones every year while Black Spruces hold onto theirs for decades. White Spruce, Black Spruce, what have you to tell us about waiting & acting, keeping & letting go? I savour a plum, then throw its pit into the water.

4

In a forest opening, in a sparkling pond, three girls in black, Larkspur-blue & Wild-Rose-pink bikinis go under, surface, turn on their backs. On mountain bikes, three boys in helmets & visors plummet down a precarious trail, skid to a stop, & watch. Do any of them know the word "nymphs"? At the trailside, Buffalo Beans nod their yellows in a breeze, & a perky Robin cocks its tail one, two, three times.

5

While chicken barbecues, Greg recalls his obese-breasted birds limping & toppling over, & the time a skunk slipped into the coop & killed them all. Then he gets us laughing at the night he found a mouse in the feed trough, the shadow of its head frightening on the blank walls, the ears enormous. Hours later, near sleep, I imagine genetically ballooned mice stalking through the dark & lording it over the farm.

6

To be the reconfiguration of a horse called Cyclone! To be made from two miles of barbed wire! To have no flesh, hair or blood yet suggest all the bucking power that defeated 129 riders at the Stampede! To be "all horse" yet also all wire! To be like swords turned into ploughshares, spears into pruning hooks! To kick high, as if unsubjugated, two legs & hoofs in the air—but wire, barbed wire!

Jeff De Boer's *Barbed Wire Bronco* (2006) is in the Glendow Museum in Calgary.

7

A Blackfoot story: a torn-moccasined woman hunting for firewood
heard singing & found the source was a shimmering gem, which
sang it was both medicine & charm. The next day a herd of buffalo
wandered near, so the gem was named iniskim—buffalo stone. But
a geologists' story also turns in my fingers: the gems, ammolites, are
fossilized ammonite shells. Jackets of the living became rock.

    Derived from a plaque in the Glenbow Museum.

8

Let's hear it for Leonard, the feisty bantam rooster so black beside
the plump white chickens. Too lean & muscled to be slaughtered,
he'd flap his wings at Diefenbaker the black lab, rush at us & attack
our ankles. His motto: *Be Leonard.* The night a skunk massacred the
chickens, Leonard hid behind a crate. But the chaos was too much.
The great entertainer—who untied our laces with his beak—died of
fright.

9

The waters of Johnston Canyon fall & fall & fall in the cycle from
cloud to mountaintop to lake to stream to cascade to cloud. In
the highest heights stale snow glints while in the canyon depths
a submerged Dipper walks under ripples, nostrils shut, special
lids secure over its eyes. Though small & brown, the Dipper is an
affirming, durable bird misted every day by spray from the falls'
unbroken violence.

10

In a city that includes Crowchild Trail, Many Horses Road, Chestnut Walk, Cactus Ridge, Hidden Creek Crescent, Hawkwood Boulevard, Applebrook Circle, Canyon Meadows Drive, Coral Reef Link, Meadowlark Road, Sanderling Rise, Sandpiper Mews, Canoe Square, & Wilderness Place, sub-divisions grow, new glass is cut & raised, & real-estate agents' signatures multiply like sparrows' claw-prints in the overturned earth.

11

Back home in Nova Scotia

Sitting on moss & needles, I photograph a Red-bellied Polypore. Hot, thirsty, I rest, browsing through the mushroom guide. Where are you, Bleeding Agarius, Slimy Comphibius, Fetid Marasmius? I may never see you once, Amethyst Tallowgill, Cinnabar-red Chanterelle. The names make me waxwing-full-of-fermented-berries drunk. Hey, where are you, Black Earthtongue, Goldgill Navelcap, Saltshaker Earthstar?

12

Here names slip & slide. Wake-robins aren't birds, but Red Trilliums under another name. Reindeer Moss is not moss, but lichen. Meadowlarks are not larks, Nighthawks not hawks. "Rabbit"? Snowshoe Hare. "Partridge"? Ruffed Grouse. Sweetfern is a sweet-smelling shrub, not a fern. Hen-of-the-Woods, a mushroom, lays no eggs. And the Screech Owl doesn't screech but trills & whinnies. Names, slip, slide.

13

I love the names in which beings overlap & embrace. To brush past
Crowberry & Hawkweed on the way to a marsh of Cattails & Pick-
erelweed. Gooseberry, Foxberry, Bearberry: a doubled taste. A Stag
Beetle under a Staghorn Sumac. Dog-tooth Violets & Trout Lilies
on the same path. For the price of one you get two—or even three:
a Tiger Swallowtail dips down to a patch of Mouse-ear Chickweed.

14

In memoriam William Bauer

Keen on-line birder asks if the rare Tricoloured Heron "is still in
Cow Bay. I don't want to drive out & just waste gas." On a Christmas
Bird Count long ago, my friend Bill chuckled at his half-ironic ideal
of finding just one crow. If Bill's list totalled that, I can't imagine
him saying, "What a waste of gas." Expectation-tweaker, rare man,
wouldn't he have valued that singular number like a prize pinned
to his hat?

15

We were given clams fresh from the Bay of Fundy, but got too
busy to prepare them. Days later we check the bucket: the clams
have opened, their long legs extended like so many marinating
pale penises, floating in expelled grit. The kids are appalled by the
mudflats' pornography. As we empty the bucket into the compost
bin, we hear the water & molluscs sigh, *Squeamish ones, oh squea-*
mish ones.

16

The son & the mother have weathered their most tense & convoluted argument ever. Though silence has divided them all day, she now asks him to help with yard & garden work. He crisscrosses the lawn with the push-mower while she weeds the plots & inspects the perennials. Overhead the crabapple blossoms are deep pink as if anger has risen through the roots & transformed into the colour that beautifies & suffuses the petals.

17

So many circles our vision dives into. Whirlpool in bay, crater on full moon, Black-eyed Susan's central disk. Today I found a spruce trunk's perfect knot, & a beachstone round as one compass-designed, but the key circle was a grackle's yellow eye surrounded by sleek obsidian feathers. On this planet of trillions x trillions of circles, eye was meeting eye, & I was a blunt-angled figure on the bird's retina.

18

BLOONK-ADOONK, BLOONK-ADOONK, BLOONK-ADOONK! looks laughable in print—feeble translation of that camouflaged ooze-dweller's call, as I first heard it at twilight soon after my own voice had dropped. Like the submarine call of some enormous alien. American Bittern—"Thunder Pumper," "Mire Drum." Gutteral ghostliness—swampy resonance—dinosaurish glugging. If the bird were nothing but a voice, that would be enough.

19

Hemlock Ravine again—Clintonia in full bloom, their yellow bells with hints of green that might be tricks of light, but aren't. An unshaven cop in official blue strides along, glances my way—suspiciously? Is he on a car thief's trail, or looking for a lost child? Maybe he stopped to watch a spider entrap a moth, & found the trio of Cedar Waxwings with their stylish crests and black masks.

20

In a thin rain, Norway Maples drop their two-winged fruit onto the sidewalks: at sixteen I wrote a love-poem comparing such samaras to the words of a girl, who decades later died by her own hand. Then a Song Sparrow's lone voice takes me further back, to the days when I first read a 75¢ paperback of *Silent Spring*. The samaras shine in this sun-shower, but some bird might sing, "Bitter-sweet-sweet, bitter-sweet-sweet."

21

oil oil   slicked brown pelican   oil oil   flightless horned grebe   oil oil   crow-coloured vesper sparrow   oil oil   golden plover no longer gold   oil oil   magnificent frigatebird in need of a name-change   oil oil   "the water, like a witch's oils...with my cross bow / I shot the—" black-legged stilt hooded merganser   oil oil   least sandpiper even less   oil oil   fish crow now with the fishes   water water

22

First week of full-fledged leafing—branches heavier, greens denser, gaps fewer, camouflage easier. Rhodora leaves now reaching pell-mell across the footpath. Everywhere, a sands-on-the-beach plenty of leaves. Half lost in shadows, I step around a tight corner, so a startled stranger cries, "Oh I thought you were an animal!" I am, ma'am—my eyes herbivorous in the voluminous greens.

23

Outside my study window the old Beech & the old Sycamore are finally in full leaf. During bare-branched winter I glimpsed silhouetted neighbours, who must've glimpsed me too. But now the carnival of photosynthesis hides the windows & I face uncountable leaves, as if we were all tree-dwellers peering across the way, wondering if an enemy tribe lived beyond the sky-diminishing wall of green.

24

Half our frontyard is flowers & shrubs. While I guide the lawnmower around, neighbours stop & praise the proliferation. "My wife's work," I say, or "It's Karen's garden." A perfectionist, she alone complains she hasn't nearly enough time to serve it well. At dinner she's skeptical if I mention more strangers finding pleasure in the garden just as it is—swoops & tangles, fallen blossoms, all that leafy leaping over boundaries.

25

Through razor-edged reeds & gone-to-seed Cattails, two Canada Geese rest on a heat-hazed islet. We slip through the brush on the bank to see them from another angle. Geese so silent, still, grounded. Then one turns its head, & we see the gosling between them. In that instant the pair becomes a mother & father—as if we thought a poem was finished, then turned the page & found another stanza, another life.

26

No lupin for an hour, then I walk up a short knoll & find hundreds of them standing tall, or leaning one way, or broken. Some event to remember might happen here, the skeptical & the faithful gathered in grass, robed in purples, blues, pinks & yellows. Blessed are those that sing, shriek, trill. Blessed are the burrowers & the divers. Blessed are the colours that both divide up the day & make it one.

27

Beatrice, Nebraska

Through jet-lag, Sunday morning in small-town Nebraska: a hedge fidgetty with sparrows, a dove floating prolonged "o"s into the air, a watering-can left on the grass, bells sounding from blocks away to the transformatively slowed-down tune of "Glory, glory, hallelujah." If you erased the cars, & the bells rang from a Buddhist temple, would Basho—flown in from 17th-century Japan—feel at home?

28

Three years ago when we first strolled along this field, my daughter slipped away into corn so tall that we lost sight of her for a minute. But this year it's the turn of beans, which don't grow high enough to hide anyone. Laura is nearly ten now, & the crops' backing-&- forthing doesn't parallel her life's riverine reach. But as long as memory lasts, I'll never forget her disappearing amidst the corn.

29

Cadaver dogs finally found the young man who drowned the other day swimming in the high fast water of the muddy river. He left behind a one-year-old. Diane says he was "a daredevil"—so was the river a devil daring him? If yes, wouldn't it be a god too? When the son is older, some days may he swim happily in the Big Blue River, even if his deepest maps always know it as The River That Drowned My Father.

30

This evening of lawnchairs I recall an Italian carving of Man at the top of Creation & all other creatures below. Over the garden early fireflies spark, & a little higher a robin settles back onto her under-eaves nest. Cicadas crackle-buzz in the trees. Bats dart higher still, yet far below bug-nabbing swifts. Nine vultures— strengthened by the guts of the dead—ride on air currents to which no other birds climb.

JULY

...woods or moods?...

1

Smack-dab in the middle of the U.S. on July 1st, ask what should be Canada's National Bird. Where the Bald Eagle rules, "no" to another charismatic-megafauna choice. What about the Grey Jay—Canada Jay, Moosebird, Whiskeyjack? When I've handed them hunks of bread on ski trails, hasn't something like wit flashed in their eyes? For *Perisoreus canadensis* let's claim a corner of the sky-blossoming fireworks back home.

2

Today I walked through an oxymoron in Lincoln: Wilderness Park. Yet a Cardinal sang its crystalline notes, & White-breasted Nuthatches called from here, Marsh Wrens from there. I caught myself thinking, "Like an aviary," then crossed out the simile. Yellow-throated Vireos, withholding their sweeter sounds, kept rasping in the branches, like children running in circles shaking rainsticks as fast as they could.

3

Stuck to the cement pillar-props of an overpass, dozens of mud nests like rows of mini-caves. Cliff Swallows fly into & out of the sun—so while watching, you shade your eyes, & the ever-so-quick swallows turn into silhouettes. Are birds with such flight-freedom well on their way to spirit? But they catch flies that are mostly wing, then swoop back to the underpass & feed them to their troglodyte chicks.

4

My first Killdeer was by Passamaquoddy Bay, N.B., its name hand-
ed to me like an heirloom by my grandmother while she peered
through her binoculars. Over the decades hundreds of Killdeer
followed in my home region—but today in the Great Plains a
pair skimmed over a beanfield & let out their sharp cries. My first
thought was "What are *you* doing here?" Note that in *The Book of
Kinds of Ownership We Need to Give Up.*

5

Abandoned farm: we swing open the rusted gate into the spaces
where pigs once ate, drank, mated & slept. Our sandals cross cement
upon which trotters tapped. Troughs are still there, & numbered
sections, & shelters from rain & wind. But when I breathe in deeply,
I can't smell the least trace of the pigs. Imagine all such pens
likewise empty, & only the ghosts of pigs roaming—some day that
will be our story too.

6

With his mighty-muscled Nebraskan cousins, Josh earns $100 U.S.
lifting & throwing hay-bales in the heat. Two days later, we're in the
Art Institute of Chicago gazing at Monet's glowing *Haystacks.* We
should return to that farm south of Lincoln & linger at dawn, dusk,
& noon by the sharp-scented, bristling bales ignited with red or
golden light, edged by brown or blue shadows.

7

Sad with incompleteness, the gallery grieves that it houses only six of Monet's *Haystacks*, the others far-flung, in Boston, New York, L.A., London, Edinburgh, Paris, Zurich. Would give my right foot to visit a vast room where all the twenty-five canvasses hang—a field where the hours & seasons are shoulder to shoulder, & light shifts spaces & plays changing tricks every few yards amidst the shorn hay.

8

He anxiously observes the differences that occur from minute to minute, & is the artist who sums up meteors & elements in a synthesis. He tells tales of mornings, noondays, twilights; rain, snow, cold, sunshine—the uninterrupted flow of changing & interrelated sensations...the possibility of summing up the poetry of the universe within a circumscribed space. Pieces of the planet take shape on his canvases.

Rearranged translation of commentary by Gustave Geffroy in May 1891 catalogue for the exhibition of Monet's *Haystacks* series.

9

Did our bodies trap Great Plains heat & bring it back here to coastal Nova Scotia? Swampy humidity, heatwave, day-long headaches— but ants scramble in the sand, an unfazed Cabbage Butterfly flutter-tilts over the hedge, & a Red Squirrel utterly free of vertigo breezes from branch tip to fence top as if to say, *Brother, this heat's not gonna get* me *down while you disappear into the white noise of fans.*

10

Butter dots the family's fingers & chins, bright as blood on a wolf family's muzzles & paws. Earlier, by the swimming pool, the parents & their children posed with the lobsters in their hands, still alive. The gas-flamed pot of water coming to a boil, the black-taped claws didn't move. While the camera's shutter clicked like some other crustacean, the family grinned widely & the thick antennae stirred the air.

11

In Shakespeare By The Sea's tongue-in-cheek *Treasure Island*, an unrehearsed Tiger Swallowtail flap-zags through a sword-fight. Since the blades are styrofoam, it comes to no harm. While Long John Silver's puppet parrot squeaks, "By Thunder!" a distant White-Throated Sparrow sings a song from long before the centuries of pirates. Its voice and the butterfly's flight are only two nuggets of the afternoon's gold.

12

In our back shed in mid-July, behind bicycles, shovels & winter tires: the snowshoes from my thirteenth Christmas. The day I first walked web-footed in a forest, a buckle tore apart, so I then staggered & ploughed, slowly, with the gift under my arm, through panic & mountainous snow. Back on the road hours later, my feet were chilled with night. That New Year's Day is still caught like a pine needle in the webbing.

13

Anyone in a living-room or restaurant gnawing their fingernails or painstakingly picking at an elbow scab drives me to distraction— yet this morning in the woods a stranger sitting on a rock working away at his toenails, busy as a shoemaker bent to his labours, didn't faze me. Did I keep calm because he wasn't within walls, but on his own, relaxing where beetles crisscrossed a mouse's corpse & a feral cat rubbed its claws on tree bark?

14

At dusk in the seaside park, our white frisbee floats & dips two last times—mother to daughter to father—like a slice of the full moon. A pair of Mourning Doves offer a one-note elegy to the day. In the container port, illuminated cranes taller than Tyrannosaurus Rexes keep working, & will until the dawn & beyond. Oh how terrible to be a crane lifting great weights, we say on our drive home, & never know sleep!

15

Would you call our compost bin a temple for these House-flies (Driveway-flies, Backyard-flies)? With 65 million more years under its belt than *Homo sapiens*, this insect once wore the armor of Beelzebub. Yet what devil sleeps in the dark, like us, & only lives a fortnight or a month? In their brief frantic lives, these swarming ones accept our mildewed bread, squashed tomatoes, & teeth-nicked cantaloupe rinds.

16

Dozens of cars travel ninety minutes to an open-air theatre. While the play's Puritan girls, shrieking, dance like one-winged pheasants, real Goldfinches scout the forest edges. Jury machinations revolve: a distant Ovenbird calls *Teacher, teacher, teacher!* Homeward bound, a driver sees a raccoon's eyes flare red in the headlights, hears a hard thunk—did the theatre gods need a blood sacrifice to complete the night?

17

In the dark as we drive home from the Valley, Laura calls out from the back seat, "Did you know a dolphin's brain is always half awake & half asleep—so the brain never gets tired?" Does that finned fact from one of her winter school-days then slip back into her memory's blue depths? When I glance far above the highway, I'm not sure how much of my brain sees a dolphin-shaped cloud arcing over the moon.

18

wind or mind? bear or hear? mild or wild? wiry or airy? peaks or freaks? drought or draught? endless or budless? expensive or expansive? command or commend? carting or casting? wearing or weaving? flaming or flowing? humble or bumble? reason or season? fertility or futility? world or worlds? me or one? woods or moods? almost or utmost?

> Selections from editors' uncertain transcriptions of words in the manuscripts of Thoreau's 1848-53 journals.

19

In a shrub on Oxford Street, the shabbiest pair of Blue Jays we've ever seen: wings & crests askew, hangover fuzziness around the eyes. Have these raptor-mimics scrapped with a Crow gang, or swallowed rotten eggs? Their elegance & whippersnappish moods should return, but their bedraggled selves attract us—like wind-ripped, buffetted Wild Roses no less beautiful than roses pristine on the first day of full blooming.

20

From a spruce top a Robin haltingly sings, & a Mourning Dove calls from as high up in a tamarack while a Crow opens & shuts its wings in another spruce's crown. Even a Chickadee flutters in the highest branch of a birch. Why does every bird this evening stick to the heights? Only the most grounded of us could guess this has something to do with transfiguration, an imminent rising into higher reaches.

21

In increments a restless Kingbird moves down a telephone wire, regularly lifts off & lands, & a Monarch Butterfly brushes against Queen Anne's Lace. Did the Victorians come up with such names? In Manhattan, writing about New Brunswick forests, Sir Charles God Damn Roberts called a moose "King of the Mamozekel." But this isn't, Sir, buddy, the British Empire any more. Queen Anne's Lace by its other name: Wild Carrot.

22

Clinging to tall grasses & clover stems, a scattered condominium built of bubbles. Spittlebugs, those Froghopper nymphs, excreted soapy liquid into which the bellows in their abdomens pumped air. Hidden, covered in their own foam, they now drink the plants' juices—but I only know this, don't see it with my eyes. I brush past the clover without stopping to knock on the doors of those houses of froth.

23

Though a lover of shade, shelter & night, a Red-bellied Snake curves through sunlit grasses. I tread softly, but it must feel the shocks of my weight & pace—slides away. Earlessness has its compensations. Imagine picking up such minute rhythms down your body's length. To feel Bach or Monk in your nerve-endings as that snake feels your footsteps—to be all ear & know this contrapuntal place head to foot!

24

Just below my knee, a bump the size of a small apple swells: a Horse-fly's work, livid rose, like an inoculation gone bad. I hardly have the hide of a horse. Does the insect's name mean it hangs around horses, or has the bite of one? While my skin flares & itches, another winged stinger rattles against leaves. Horse-fly, Horse-fly, if I wrote as many poems about you as Issa did about flies & crickets, would you scram?

25

If a tumour is swelling on your body, you should dampen an amethyst with your saliva & touch the tumor all over with it. Whose ears are ringing should take winter cherry, daub it on felt, & place that felt around his neck, up to his ears. If you dry a blackbird's liver & always carry it with you, the devil will not torment you. Who becomes weak in his heart should pulverize whale's heart & drink it in water.

Sentences selected & adapted from *Physica* by Hildegaard von Bingen (1098-1179), translated by Priscilla Throop from the Latin.

26

For eight generations beekeeping has been in the family's blood, but now the insects' numbers are shrinking, & nobody can capture the reason why. Gold & black & silver, the Honey Makers are dying, turning the colour of mud. The Great Pollinators fall from the sky or from their hives—poisoned or chilled promises, doomed hopes—& stay-at-home pollen lingers like millions of unsent messages with no messenger.

27

Combinations, combinations! A Yellowthroat calls *Witchery, witchery, witch!* while pale fuzzy Meadowsweets bathe in 9 a.m. light. As shadows peel from Evening Primroses, a Red-winged Blackbird plucks a purpling red berry from a Shadbush. My wondering why Shadbush is also *Service*berry intersects with memories of Stan Getz's tenor sax—light-winged enough to be an alto. Combinations, combinations, newborn every minute...

28

Sharpest contrast today on the Bluff Wilderness Trail: star-like yellow blossoms on tall stalks—then waxy white transluscencies, strangers to chlorophyl, on the forest floor. The former fulfilled one floral archetype—sun-coloured blossoming—while the latter, parasitic on others' roots, held up their own oddness, spurning flowerhood. The Indian Pipes burn in memory just as intensely as the Swamp Candles.

29

The new members of our household—a month old, one charcoal, one tabby grey—experiment with wrestling, thread-tugging, & shoulder-climbing, their gait like a saddle-sore cowboy's. In the forest I come across a young toad, its brown skin spotted with black-edged orange. It too hobbles & lurches; a tree root, like a ridge in a blanket, poses a problem. Through their imbalances the four-legged ones learn.

30

Framed in a church basement window, Laura & other dancers finish the day's free-form, jazz & hip-hop classes. A web spun across the glass hints at the abandoned, the decaying & the haunted—then I see the jiggling dots of baby spiders, & the web no longer contradicts the dancers but confirms them. Past the complex threads, Laura scoops the air with both hands & throws imaginary grains.

31

Between the trail & the skinny river a sign: STEEP DROP. Here & there, much trickier inclines—so why the warning where none is needed? Such shouting of danger straightens too many walks, & discourages detours leading to the places you'll remember most—like the gully with moisture-beaded Sundews & a pair of Meadowhawk dragonflies poised on a rock & linked in a mating wheel.

AUGUST

...sharp whistles distinctly different...

1

Fredericton

Along the riverbank Angelica thrives like flowers that have a hankering to be trees—six feet tall, with branching, purple, celeryish stems & dusty-white heads. Tropical wildness in a butterfly-luring place where six months later snow will encompass everything, as if the weather took an exaggerated hint from the blossoms' white. In the meantime we could rename The City of Stately Elms The City of Swaying Angelica.

2

For Karen, on her birthday

My ladybird, today it is rainy, cold & horrid. My dear goldfish, greetings. Poppet, linnet, two letters have come from you today. I embrace my heron—my little whale. My darling German pony—my incomparable pony. I didn't telegraph "cross dog" but "sweet" dog, they must have got it wrong in the telegraph office. My joy, very wise dog—my marmot, splendid creature—crocodile of my soul!

> A collage of salutations from Anton Chekhov to his wife, Olga Knipper, in letters written between 1898 & 1904, translated by Constance Garnett from the Russian.

3

Walking in a forest where I walked so often when I was his age, my son asks, Don't you hate it when you reach up & find a dead bug caught in your hair? Are there moose in here? Are caribou deer? When will we get back to the car? Why are cheetahs faster than lions? What are you taking a picture of? What's the difference between a lake & a pond? If I threw a rock in, would the tadpoles start swimming? Do those lilies grow in the ocean too?

4

Far past midnight, I wake to the clicking of crickets, which hear each other with their knees' timpanic membranes. In Queen Square tennis balls & softballs have given way to those insects running a wingtip along the comb-like veins on their opposite wing's underside. While calls around the world ring—Cave Crickets, Sand Crickets, Jerusalem Crickets—I lie awake, running one big toe along the toes of my other foot.

5

The plump body of a turkey behind a fence at King's Landing is feathered in uninterrupted white, so we quickly go to the red wattle, the beak's hint of yellow, the Pre-Raphaelite blue around the eyes. Months away, Thanksgiving is an X on a calendar, a cataclysm in the offing. Whoever slices into the gobbler's headlessness with knife & fork will know too little of this body warmed by sunlight in its feathers.

6

Lightning splits the sky & thunder thuds like giant boulders rolling down a hill. The atmosphere has downtimes but keeps returning to its conflicts. I retell the tale of the Thunders asking Mosquito where tasty blood was. "Mosquito greedily tricked them into trying granite, pine, brookwater, the sea." When our windows rattle, thunder is getting closer to the real delicacy, the feast running through our veins.

A version of the Mi'kmaq tale summarized above is found in Ruth Holmes Whitehead's *Stories from the Six Worlds: Micmac Legends.*

7

Just past Harvey Station, a half-acre of Goldenrod—stalks of splintered light, spears of yellow fire. As we drive past, King Midas seems to have stirred awake from centuries of sleep long enough to touch the field with one finger. Then the half-acre shakes, living rather than still gold. The Ancients sink back into our subconscious: the Goldenrod multiplies amidst all the green, lit with presence, rooted & rising.

8

We don't have to see a swarm of krill or fish to know one is there. In Passamaquoddy Bay, the signs meet in one misshapen circle: Sooty & Greater Shearwaters, afloat or in flight—Harbour Porpoises surfacing for a second—a Finback Whale's dorsal fin sliding that way. At an observation boat's railing, we too take part, but distantly, with an appetite for watching all those appetites converge in the furious water.

9

Not far from porpoises snuffling & whining, nearly every inch of a rocky islet bared at low tide is furred with Harbour Seals. Mottled tan, dark brown, or silvery, they rest flank to flank, flipper to whiskers—black concave eyes fixed on our boat. Those rocks are so popular that three room-starved seals slip into the water, but they won't remain satellites: they'll return, their blunt noses insisting on a place to be both stubborn and languid.

10

On the drive from New Brunswick to Nova Scotia, I gaze up & watch clouds travelling above the Tantramar Marshes. Cumulus masses, grand confections of waterdrops & air, drift in the blue 6000 feet up. Three times higher, ice-crystal Cirrus horses' tails are splayed, closer to abstraction. I'm ready to stick up my dukes to my Albertan friends & say, "Big Sky Country is where you find it."

11

Imaginary folk sayings

If you stare into a raven's eye for more than a minute, you'll get a sore throat / Don't eat the meat of a crab caught between midnight & dawn, or you'll have nightmares of drowning / If an artist picks a bouquet of devil's paintbrushes, the toxins of his paints will sicken him / The child who rescues a grasshopper from a wading-pool without breaking its legs will become a champion gymnast

12

At the International Busker Festival, thousands of mating ants fly in & cram the air, driving audiences indoors. A fire-eater shrugs, a living statue flinches, a contortionist halts. If the ants were big as gulls, they'd be the day's highlight—dodging lamp-posts, catching in sails, pyrotechnically linking above the boardwalk with precision a mid-air acrobat would envy. Who will hold out a hat for the flying ants?

13

More imaginary folk sayings

If you crush more than ten raspberries under your feet, the bush will be bare next summer / A red fox running past a white church means a friend has just gone into the hospital / Let a kite-eating tree claim your flying dragon, & vertigo will dog your days / If your cat eats a yellow warbler, the sun will disappear for a week / Tell someone to leave a spider alone, & you will be blessed eight times

14

Big Tancook Island

Last night the sky over this island of few lights revealed more stars than the sky over our backyard at home ever has. Likewise, though we stroll past a giant satellite dish luring a channel-changer's Babel, today local sounds travel clearly, as if the island granted us superior ears—voices & laughter from the wharf, a sheep's bleat, each stride of a distant young woman slowly wading into the shallows of Southeast Cove.

15

On this island three miles long—paved road, one B&B, two school-rooms—spacious, rolling lawns are kept tidy & shorn, but I'm drawn to the lanky grasses & flowers spreading over a rust-ravaged tractor wheel. Wildness crowds an antique fire-engine & the flaking shell of a Pentecostal church. The eye delights in rot & reckless fertility, Bull Thistles & Goldenrod burying a rocking-horse forgotten in a field.

16

Fishing nets strung from poles surround Tancook's gardens. An old man on the road talks about an "epidemic" of deer. In hunting season last fall, eighty were shot, so I imagine families nourished through the winter with the leaves of their own carrots & cauliflower transformed into venison. "Funny," says the stranger, "how what we planted came back to us"—that full circling making the corners of his mouth lift into a grin.

17

If someone is overwhelmed by numbness, another should take a bit of earth from the right & left side of the bed, & from near the person's right & left foot. While digging he should say, "You, earth, are sleeping in this person." When the earth is placed under the patient's head & feet, this should be said, "You, earth, grow & be useful in this person, so that he may receive your greenness, in the name of—"

Abridged from a passage in *Physica* by Hildegard von Bingen (1098-1179), translated by Priscilla Throop from the Latin.

18

Once in my early teens I cradled a dead Star-nosed Mole in the palm of my hand. The fur was shockingly soft, like fallen, browned rose petals. My fingers tingled, as if with electricity. The nose radiated like an exotic organ evolved inside the earth for aeons—fleshy evidence that our lawn was the grassy roof of another world, or of an earthly stratum to which we'd never given a passing thought.

19

Cape Breton Island

Outside Louisbourg we hike along one of Earth's unacknowledged borderlands, between the realms of the snake-necked seabirds and the ursine rambler. On volcanic off-shore rocks a dozen cormorants take turns spreading their wings widely like dark fine-meshed screens to dry in the light. Turning from the basalt-coloured birds, we find on the footpath basalt-coloured bear shit laced with blueberries.

20

Bent over among the rocks in Wolfe Cove, we find the remains of many sea urchins, most of them minus their spines. Their shells' 5 radiating bands reveal their 5 feet, 5 gonads, & 5-sided chewing mechanism ("Aristotle's lantern") digested by gulls, ducks or lobsters. Hours later in a downtown pub a stranger asks what we did today, & we offer a baffling answer: "Searched high & low for Aristotle's lantern."

21

On the horizon at Dominion Beach, a sign of conflicting times: the towers of wind-power generators lined up on either side of a coal-burning plant. White blades slicing, black smoke rising. Late August, Yellow-rumped Warblers fidget among thicknesses of Myrtle, the seeds so plentiful the birds won't answer the familiar calls to migrate. Once named Myrtle Warblers, they crack hard green seeds under the skies of Industry.

22

Riding a bus, I glimpse a Belted Kingfisher beating its blue-grey wings fast over the deeper blue of the Bras d'Or Lakes. Instantly it disappears, as if our fate were to run on parallel lines for less than a second, not even crossing paths. From far below this ridge, it couldn't have seen me. How many million times have *I* been the fleeting object in eyes that merely caught sight of me, then sped on their way?

23

During Clam Harbour's Sand Castle & Sculpture Day, we find—all more arresting than any castle—an enchanted cobra, a whippet, a labyrinth, & a Mad Hatter. Two dolphins leap into the air, yet they're made of sand & attached to the beach. By the glittering grains, we squint & see a kayak-sized dragonfly about to vibrate its wings free, rise over our hats & bald spots & hot hair & rattle away, showering sand upon us all.

24

On a crumbly seaside bank, grand stalks of Mullein—3' high, velvety upright leaves & few yellow blossoms—shift arrhythmically in the wind. I was going to say they're like defiant towers, but no god decides they need to be humbled by having their language dispersed into a Babel of many. While sailboats in the background skim past, the Mulleins hold deep-rootedness together with changeable motion.

25

Over shrubby land near a girls' soccer tournament, a Northern Harrier lets out sharp whistles distinctly different from the referees'. Aloft on dihedral-angled wings, she stays distant from the goalposts, the girls & the speeding ball. When the field is abandoned, the Harrier still has scant interest in this consistent green: long ago she must've cut out the astroturf from her map of places worth attention & appetite.

26

Today on the outskirts of Stewiacke, Laura, you gripped the edge of a sign marking a mid-point between North Pole & Equator. "I wouldn't want to live in either," you said, "just visit." We're lucky to taste both—sweat & shiver, go barefoot & big-booted, track through burning beach-sand & waist-high snow. While you sleep now, I wish you dreams of an Armadillo & a Snowy Owl.

27

During our drive from Halifax to Truro, suddenly the highway is red. Road-builders turned ever-changing tidal mud from nearby Cobequid Bay into long-lasting hardness. Speeding over ordinary blackness again, we imagine other highways infused with local colour: asphalt green from a bordering forest, or rich brown from a field often tilled, or (the distant heights captured & extracted) blue, from the overarching sky.

28

Munroes Island, Northumberland Strait. Three Black-headed Gulls shift in the waves near the sand where three Ruddy Turnstones, finely patterned in russet & black, follow the shoreline: a roll-of-the-dice species-combination new to me. Farther along, a Willet nimbly steps around a Rock Crab's broken remains: another novel mix. Before leaving the beach to resume other roles, how fulfilling just to witness.

29

Beside the pies in Masstown Market, Rosaria & Darlene say they hoped to pick blueberries yesterday near their house, but found a feasting bear. Each time they returned, the beast was still gobbling; hours later it sank, satisfied, & slept. I buy a blueberry pie. Back home, my family elsewhere, I eat one slice—two—three. Finally I collapse on the couch, full-bellied, berry-drugged, purple-tongued.

30

Just a silhouette & a voice are sometimes enough. Evening, the hottest August 30th in memory, by Governor's Lake three Cedar Waxwings on three branches, their colours lost in their silhouettes' black. Those slurred sounds seem too private to be "calls." Then, the shape of a canoe, three outlined strangers speaking low. Clearly it's an evening for tête-à-têtes, & broadcasts must wait for cooler days.

31

Yesterday "a slowly moving cluster of thunderstorm cells" (thanks, National Weather Service) worked its way through the Annapolis Valley, setting MacIntosh & Honeycrisp Apples free, only to roll & bruise them on the ground. One vineyard lost 25% of its crop to grape-sized hailstones. Terse on the telephone to a radio reporter, a worker offered these words, like three grapes or three hailstones: "This is nature."

SEPTEMBER

...onto the asymmetrical sea...

1

Ireland

Dalkey Island (Thorn Island) is home to fifteen or twenty feral goats: close enough that I'm squinting across the waves, trying to spot one of the horned, hardy beasts. With no other mammals except rabbits & rats, the island suggests a truncated future—but if the water were calmer, I could hire a boat & be the fourth species. Excavation of a neolithic midden there once revealed a human skull full of ritual periwinkles.

2

Along Sandymount Strand south of Dublin, the tide is at its lowest low. A couple of Hooded Crows rise from behind purple Alfalfa & red bursts of Valerian. Among a few Oystercatchers rushing across mud, a Black-tailed Godwit feeds, preoccupied but elegant. If I kept a birder's Life List that species would be given a number, but I don't tag it with a statistic, & instead wonder if some early monk decided birds were creations of God's wit.

3

After we walk past vans painted with a cartoonish, chubby monk eating his fill—KEVIN'S KITCHEN, KEVIN'S CONES—our guide tells us that St. Kevin stood so long in a lake with his arms outstretched that birds built nests in his hands. Glendalough in County Wicklow has given us that tale of supreme service & patience. Who among us could remain motionless in many weathers until a finch wound grasses through our fingers?

4

On a Dublin sidewalk a carved, life-sized lion is chained—oh to be wooden yet still chained! I laugh when a carter asks Beckett's Mrs. Rooney if she wants a load of dung, & she answers, "Dung? What class of dung?" In a sparsely blossomed shrub in St. Stephens Green, a single blossom hanging alone reminds me of the proverbial lost sheep. Inside a window saying INTERNATIONAL YEAR OF BIODIVERSITY, no lights are on.

5

By a lake an angel appeared to St. Kevin & said, "In your afterlife your soul will oversee fifty living monks." When the prediction of that small number disappointed Kevin, God's messenger went on, "Then a great city shall rise here, should the four mountains making this valley be levelled into rich meadows." But the monk shook his head & said, "All the creatures of the mountains are my housemates," & the mist swallowed his complaint.

6

As the plane back to Canada lifts into the air, I open *The Irish Times* & read about "re-introduced" birds of prey: Golden Eagles (from Scotland), Red Kites (from Wales), White-tailed Sea Eagles (from Norway). Despite deaths from poisoned carcasses meant for foxes, those newcomers multiply. Their living, flexible wings—so different from the stiff metal wings outside the cramped windows up here.

7

On the sidewalk I meet our young neighbours' daughter, three weeks old, sleeping in her mother's arms. The father says she was born on a day of consecutive thunderstorms, when sharp changes in barometric pressure sent more pregnant women than usual into labour. "Surreal," I whisper—then, as the infant's eyes open, I know neither parent needed lightning-charged hours to feel earth & air transformed.

8

Beyond Sambro Island, twenty kilometres out to sea, I "saw" a Manx Shearwater for the first time. Or the avian afficianado I've heard has "the sharpest eyes in the province" called out, "Manx Shearwater!" Then for less than a second I managed to spot a dark, long-winged bird rushing over distant sun-dazzled crests & troughs. But did I *see* a Manx Shearwater? I glimpsed one—or even less, was *told* I glimpsed one.

9

After we flung mackerel & popcorn (yes, popcorn: it's white, it floats) from the boat, a trio of Northern Fulmars were the first to arrive—blunt-billed white seabirds, dark feathers like smudged mascara under their eyes. Cackling, they fed until their big cousins, Herring Gulls, took over—then, beggars who can't be choosers, they opted for the popcorn. I let out a mock-gull laugh when one stubborn Fulmar won the race to a mackerel.

10

No gulls or dogs at Chocolate Lake, but mobbed sunbathers & swimmers, an inflated plastic turtle & sea-horse, & tattoos, tattoos! Hawk's head on a leather-vested motorcyclist's shoulder—black stallion running across a young woman's smooth belly—green snake curled around an ankle—Morpho Butterfly spreading its blue across a puckered, aging back. What a motley ink-burned menagerie!

11

Another morning of dew—droplets on the Wild Rose heads, on the Beach-pea petals, at Fisherman's Cove. Dew often takes me back to Issa's haiku on his daughter's death from smallpox, after his two sons had already lived too briefly: *The dewdrop world / is the dewdrop world / & yet...& yet.* Trying to console himself by saying the transitory is our bedrock. The Beach-pea world is the Beach-pea world—& yet...& yet—

Haiku translated by Robert Hass from the Japanese.

12

A dragonfly too fast to be ID'd skims over a patch of Spotted Touch-Me-Nots. If everything living were that restless, how long would our patience last? When the winged elude us, the rooted remain: our eyes then settle on those pouches of freckled orange, & the frothy pinks of Meadowsweet, & the greenish white umbels of Wild Carrots drying out, preparing for the day they drift free, turned into miniature tumbleweeds.

13

As Hurricane Ed gets closer, a Chickadee on a branch doesn't sing—sensing mayhem less than a day away? Climate junkies, how you hunker down to The Weather Network, caught between wishing for a calm anti-climax & wanting Ed (friendly-sounding name) to rip through the city & make a few stories out of uprooted trees, shattered windows, scattered roofs, & statues decapitated by iconoclastic winds.

14

Earlier I'd called the hurricane Ed, but by the time he got here today I had his name right. Earl pulled crab apples off the tree & flung them across the patio, buried a bus-shelter under a fallen tree, crowned a parked car with snapped power-lines. More boisterous uncle than monomaniacal pater—but I saw great old maples with great branches torn off, their pale, pale inner wood bared, left new & vulnerable.

15

While the hurricane gusted & flower pots rocked, I pulled a book by Ammons off a shelf & randomly read how a wind-propelled leaf could "tell a good / deal about / big affairs, volumes, / currents, long / tugs, ascensions, / wheels"—words utterly of the moment. Chance was apt & funny. The book was *Worldly Hopes*, the poem "Extravaganza." Hearing & watching billowing branches, I had no interest in unworldly hopes.

16

Wanting to prove the harbour is clean, in yellow & black swim-shorts the Mayor wades in, then goes underwater. Reporters & other citizens gaze. The new sewage-treatment plant, costing $54-million, broke down last year—bad press. To drown bad press with good press, the Mayor gets wet in his bumblebee-striped suit. In the water he keeps his lips shut perfectly tight.

17

Poring over photos of last week's Fulmars (who are surely this week's Fulmars too), I see what I didn't see at the time: the ways the rocking water broke up their shapes & features in its mirrorings. The complete birds were wave-riding & feeding, but my eyes were drawn to the fragments of them—a half-wing here, a breast there, an eye floating alone—thrown onto the asymmetrical sea. The sea is a restless Cubist.

18

As if all the tombstones in the region said *Waste Not, Want Not*, evaporated rainwater ascends to blend into new clouds, crows tear off chunks of a dead woodchuck, & a spiderweb in an abandoned birdfeeder works it stickiness on bugs. Near the beach, in a robin's ex-nest, a mouse has given birth. The tiny cries aren't interrupted by a landlord's or landlady's knock, & no fussy lease awaits a belated signature.

19

On his walk through the Captain Arnell Lands soon after the fire, David recalled "Black Is The Colour of My True Love's Hair." But last year over this granite bedrock, scorching heat released the seeds of twisty-branched Jack Pines, so now we find seedlings higher than our ankles. In the Conflagration or the Inferno, would all be lost if Jack Pines were around, opening the scales of their cones, feeding the ashes?

20

Leaning against the house, a plastic bag labelled GREENWORLD / COMPOSTED SHEEP MANURE, unopened but for the tear a flowerless plant made from the inside, so desperate was its need to burst the bounds of being mere fertilizer. Did its original seed spend hours in a sheep's guts? From a wide crack in the cement steps, Red Clover still blooms. Whether four-leaf or not, does it hint at good fortune?

21

During the black-out I told bored Josh to explore the neighborhood. He half-teased, "Dad, anyone who goes walking alone is a loser." Guess I was a loser at puberty, a loser at thirty, a loser at fifty, & I'm still a loser. Not every day. Sometimes Karen & I walk where a red leaf falls like a tiny meteor & Cotton Grass tufts, smudged moons, glow. But even alone, I feel like a winner, given the forest at dusk & my dearest ones not far away.

22

Lightly scratched into three boulders along a mile in Hemlock Ravine: KJD. Though no enthusiast of carving names into trees, I'm happy to find those KJDs: someone shares those initials with my Karen. Defacement turns into love-talismans, like barley mordifords left by peasant lovers for each other. Would any other initials make me so forgiving of the hand with the jackknife or key?

23

An hour after teaching "Pied Beauty" by Hopkins: blandly named Point Pleasant, this park now in September could be Pied Beauty Park, with many green leaves already dappled brown under the couple-coloured sky, pathways stippled with fallen berries & brinded with snapped twigs, leading to the beach where young gulls are counter & freckled. Nothing here may be past change, but is anything past praise?

24

"Butterflies have withdrawn from flight," I thought not long ago, but too early. Since then, Clouded Sulphurs have flicked past in pale yellow, & a Mourning Cloak relaxed its purple-brown wings on hole-ridden Bunchberry leaves. The only almanac worth composing includes inaccurate dates. If I ever had a crystal ball, by now it would be sharded & thrown into a stream, swift water rushing over the pieces of its certainties.

25

In the rain a man walks his dog in its fringed yellow cape. Innocent enough—yet think of Reality-TV dogs groomed, dyed, chalked, & transformed into dog-tigers, dog-horses, dog-iguanas—then you have genetic engineers in their steely labs trying to devise new species. Oh yes, just a dog in a downpour, but I wish the wavy fur was undraped, free to be washed by the rain.

26

Plant a satellite dish on your roof, get hooked on the Animal Channel & catch *Gang Dogs, Killer Aliens, Monsters Inside Us*! Tooth & Claw TV! Or with a magnifying glass watch the fruit flies in our homemade trap, swimming in cider vinegar under pinpricked cellophane. I made the trap, but—in case we're flies to the gods—I'm comforted by recalling how Jainists hang veils over their mouths to keep from swallowing the winged ones.

27

My favourite scene in *Rise of the Planet of the Apes*: where giant suburban trees canopy quiet streets, leaves suddenly shower down on cars & walkers. No wind thrashes: an onrush of newly intelligent creatures hurry overhead, half-flying through the high greenery. Before shock & terror kick in, surely one gazing walker thinks, "What a wonder!—the apes are free, the apes are travelling fast through the heights!"

28

Weeks after Hurricane Earl, a street in our neighbourhood is still lined with fallen branches between curb & sidewalk, all their greens gone, uniform goldy-browns awaiting decay. Tendril, root, xylem, phloem—brittle leaves cut from their beginnings. Walking with eyes down, I've entered a world without photosynthesis, the heaps of severed branches a birdless confusion, an eerie limbo.

29

I found a paddle abandoned in the woods, but no boat or raft—a rusted tin cup, but no jug of water or wine. Later, suspenders hanging from a tree, minus the pants. Farther on, a weather-bleached page—torn from its book—caught in a bed of ferns. All those findings weren't clues to a single story, but bits of many stories. Not much joined me & the strangers except the place we'd all passed through.

30

The Metamorphosis of nature shows itself in nothing more than this: there is no word in our language that cannot become typical to us of nature. The world is a Dancer; it is a Rosary; it is a Torrent; a Boat; a Mist; a Spider's Snare; the metaphor will hold, & give the imagination keen pleasure. Swifter than light the World converts itself into the thing you name. There is no thing small or mean to the soul.

Abridgement of an 1841 passage from Emerson's journals.

OCTOBER

...amidst all those maracas...

1

The bodies of my father's parents, underground for decades in Oak Bay. Today in Hemlock Ravine, in a chainsaw's wake, the fresh smells of sawdust: summers when powdery, splintery hills rose near my grandfather's mill. Then a Red-breasted Nuthatch, its slender honk: my grandmother, the first feeder-keeper I knew, put the birds' names into my ears. Sawdust, nuthatch—I finally witness their ever-renewed marriage.

2

Kudos to the fox that wandered onto the puzzling, meticulously trimmed grass of a golf course, nearly got hit by a ball, glared at the hairy-legged golfer, then trapped the ball between her teeth & transported it to the nearest sand-trap. By the time the fox vanished back into the woods like a bit of red yarn into dense fabric, she'd given the golfer a story to tell as often as any truth-stretcher about a hole-in-one.

3

St. Simeon Stylites: never a favourite of mine. Up there on a pillar 12 cubits high for 12 years—then a decade at 20 cubits high—& up to 40 cubits, on his skinny legs to the end. In old age he met a dragon suffering from a tree branch in its eye. They say he converted the beast—but I see him sliding down the slippery neck, 40 cubits down, back to the sand & grass, the rocks & flowers. In that new legend, the dragon saves the saint.

Original story found in *Beasts and Saints*, translated by Helen Waddell from the Latin.

4

Ancient sound: from across the lake, a distant hammer driving a nail into wood—surely not that different from hammer & nail in a Welsh, Corsican or Lebanese village centuries ago. That sound reaches so far back it's like a memory from a previous life, or an atavistic penetration from the time when trees were first cut down to make houses & the blacksmith-inventor of nails was still rumoured to be alive.

5

Doodled with crayons on a restaurant's brown-paper place-mat while waiting for dinner: *The quick brown fox jumps over a lazy dog. A lazy dog jumps over the quick brown fox. Over the brown dog, Lazy, jumps a fox, Quick. The quick fox-dog jumps over Lazy A. Brown. Brown Fox: ah! quick! over! jump! dog the lazy! A lazy brown dog, Jumpover, (out)-foxes the quick.*

6

Few birds, few flies, the prickle of imminent rain along the trail by the lake. Subdued & thin, today is like a scene sketched on top of seven days ago, when a hare clutched a leafy branch between its teeth, a blue feather landed on an orange leaf, & a hunched heron rose into a pink sky. Translucent evening over bold-coloured evening. This mist I walk through is like the space between two layers of a palimpsest.

7

I recall the eyes of a squirrel my grandfather shot because it was eating a robin's eggs. I sided with the squirrel—a redder spot staining its forehead—& couldn't look in my grandfather's eyes. Does each heart hold only so much pity? I didn't ask that then, hearing the rifle-shot tear the air while my grandmother (I only imagined this decades later) gently gathered bits of blue eggshell off the grass.

8

My mother's father was a bred-in-the-bone Saint Johner, a long-legged walker up & down hilly streets of the old port. One day the doorbell rang: a stranger selling shad fresh from the river. I'd never seen fish so real & complete, scales blending grey & blue & green, bright like medieval chain-mail. My grandfather bought a shad, loving the taste, but we children never had the patience to pick out the plentiful bones.

9

In Yoga class, my eyes landed on a wall-hanging of elephant-headed Ganesh, Lord of Beginnings, Remover of Obstacles, Patron of Letters & Learning—a versatile god. Why was he holding an ax? Why mounted on a rat? What was the missing tusk all about? Silent questions muffled my teacher's voice. Caught in Cobra, I was supposed to be moving into Pyramid, but Ganesh was becoming Lord of Distractions.

10

"The SunChip bags," says an AP news story, "were launched with a big marketing effort to play up their compostibility because they're made from plants & not plastic." Now Frito-Lay, hearing complaints about the rattling & crackling, withdraws the biodegradables. In Ye Olde Fickle Market, plastics have trounced plants. Frito-Lay is weak-kneed, & the SunChips I ate the other day tasted a little off & odd.

11

The half-bare branches reaching higher than our roof seem to magnetize a hundred Starlings. Those crackles & snaps sound like beach stones rolled back & forth by waves. Amidst all those maracas I also hear a few down-dipping whistles, which could be so many things: rugged-individualist jeers vs. the mob—cheers deflating at the moment of utterance—penny-whistle sighs of relief at alighting.

12

Thanksgiving weekend, a fresh flowering of Butter-and-eggs in the sand-bordered fields at MacCormack's Beach. I throw my jacket over my shoulder—zip it back on—unzip, tie it around my waist—then poke my arms up the sleeves again, body perplexed by all the switches between cool breezes and breezelessness. At the tide's edge a pair of Red Knots feed—out-of-step migrants thrown for a loop, the loop of elastic weather.

13

One day during Scarecrow Festival week in Mahone Bay, a Crow casts its eye on a patchwork Tweedledum & Tweedledee, nudges Tina Turner's purple dress, & floats its shadow over witches' plastic crows. Hear its guttural laugh? The living bird isn't silent or static, & shows no fear. As it flaps around straw-stuffed Einstein, will it tug at the black-yarned $E=mc^2$ woven across the shirt front?

14

In Chile, Los 33 rise to the earth. After two months in a collapsed gold & copper mine, one by one, thanks to a capsule named Phoenix, they rise. Have they learned as never before that deep-underground darkness isn't their home? No kin to the mole, they're reaffirmed, after a few deep breaths, as creatures of the earth's surface—but they wear dark glasses to shield their light-starved eyes from the shock of the unrelenting sun.

15

In the shallows of Frog Pond a dozen Mallards feed, tipped bottoms-up, heads & necks submerged. Miss Manners wouldn't be taken with their posture, or with the flurries of ducks that dash like children lunging at each other across the dinner table. On a shoreline bench an old man wearing a hat with a beak-like visor sways & elbows a plaintive air from the uillean pipes under his arm.

16

Since the banning of cellphone chatting & texting by drivers in Nova Scotia, 2000 have been fined. Where is *The Far Side* when we need it? Gary Larsen, please sketch this cartoon: A moose rambles down the highway, yacking into a small device strung from his antlers. As two high-beams approach from the distance, the beast—lips spread wide, teeth bared, eyes rolled back—may be laughing his final laugh.

17

A doe on the trail slips back into the forest, but doesn't flee. Neither skittish nor evasive, she browses on dangling leaves. For once, having had my fill of watching, I'm the first to go. Soon I cross paths with a white-bearded stranger & a sheepdog. Would the dog, I ask, chase deer? "Oh no," says the stranger. "Once, laying there, he didn't flinch when a doe sniffed *him* to find out what was what."

18

Stooped among beach rocks, I peer at the thread-thin reddish lines in the yellow petals of Wild Radish—then at the amassed blossoms on a Swamp Candle spike &, closer, the five petals of one, a fraction of all that clustering. Nearby a gull drops blue-black mussels onto the rocks & yanks its food from the cracked shells. Minutiae & drama, drama & minutiae—a good day, any day, overflows with both.

19

Only a narrow belt of the sky is blue, yet enough light slips through for Fraser Lake to turn smudgy gold & red, borrowing colours from the unfallen maple leaves above. Yet in the past week some of the detached leaves became waterlogged & sank to the bottom. The water will freeze & thaw, freeze & thaw. Even when the branches are bare, hints of today's red & gold—like memories of watery reflections—will linger, decaying down there.

20

Finally I see that the most moving things about autumn leaves—moving, not beautiful—are the tatters, pocks & other imperfections amidst their famous colours. Finding such marks—signs of having survived parasites & wild weather—is like hearing a hoarse singer who has lost her voice's youthful smoothness. I'm drawn to the histories suggested by such voices, as I am to the variegated, erratic-edged leaves of October.

21

In the Writer & Nature course questionnaire, I asked, *What animal do you identify with?* I got 3 cats & 2 squirrels, but just 1 dog, ferret, bear, sea otter, dolphin, sloth & penguin. The wittiest reply: *Monkey in a pointed hat.* The wisest: *tiger—dove—snake—chickadee.* Unsure what answer I would give, I gaze out at the students, trying to recall who wears that hat, & who would gladly be a bestiary.

22

News on the car radio: a 27-inch-tall Columbian, a part-time dancer in department stores, is the world's shortest man. Doctors studied him until he was three, then they "just lost interest." Mr. Hernandez complains, "People are always touching me & picking me up." Then during a harbourfront stroll, we see children gathered around a touch-tank, lifting out starfish, clams & sea cucumbers to pat & stroke.

23

It's dark outside the windows an hour before dawn while I drink tea & prepare a morning class. A jay cries, *Jeeah, jeeah, jeeah!* Have I ever heard one this early? If I caught a glimpse in moonlit trees, would it only be an unblued silhouette, a jay in the abstract? One could argue forever whether I'm hearing a cry against the dark, or a cry of the dark. So I'm relieved to think nothing but *A jay's cry, a jay's cry.*

24

Be my horses ready? ... The little dogs & all—Tray, Branch, Sweet-heart—see, they bark at me ... Though wisdom can reason thus & thus, nature finds itself scourged ... Do you owe the worm no silk, the beast no hide, the sheep no wool, the cat no perfume? ... Bless thy five wits ... o ruined piece of nature! ... through fire & flame, through ford & whirlpool, over bog & quagmire—

A collage of short passages from Shakespeare's *King Lear*.

25

Along the sides of Bridle Path, four Crows are taking a holiday from flight or learning to walk less awkwardly. The two on the right flap, stalk & hop around each other—though it's October, long past mating season. One on the left grips a chestnut in its beak, the other a crabapple. I'd not be too surprised if they nodded, then tossed their finds to each other, apple for nut, nut for apple.

26

Longest-surviving Janus cat: two-mouthed, two-nosed, three-eyed Frank & Louie gets into the *Guinness World Records*. In the eyes of Marty, who saved him from euthanasia twelve years ago, he's no longer a freak. "Every day is a blessing," she muses, stroking the luxuriant white fur. "People walk up with a big smile to pat him"—she laughs—"then a look of horror crosses their face."

27

To learn humility & be more than Lear's shadow, Lear flees to the heath, where he cries out to the wind, rain & thunder, "Here I stand your slave, a poor, bare, forked animal." Like Poor Tom, Lear's a-cold, yet he would be naked while crowned with nettles, hardocks, furrow-weeds & cuckoo-flowers. Does he offer the mouse a bit of toasted cheese to deceive & trap it—or to feed it, wretched creature to wretched creature?

28

Near the lighthouse at Chebucto Head a few drivers splattered gas over their wrecked cars, torched them & sent them rolling down a slope, blazing, into the waves. Because we believe that our origin was the ocean, it's as if those strangers returned with metal dragons, scorching the kelp & crabs, then asked their first home to swallow up those monstrous dying pets & take care of them with time & salt.

29

Despite the taxidermists' skills, the Osprey's beak looks plastic, the Black Bear's fur synthetic. The Smooth Hammerhead rests in a jar like a deformed fetus. The Sable Island horse is just its own skeleton. Yet children flock to Gus the Gopher Tortoise—alive at 88, still fond of lettuce, berries & dandelions. Then a mother-to-be enters the museum, slowly walking with the globe of her belly under her yellow dress.

30

The eye goes to the inukshuk in a stoney land, against pale blue—then moves up to five distant V's of Canada Geese. The geese are on the move, but the eye slides back to the frozen-gestured, ultra-abstracted human. Why am I pulled between the lone figure with head, legs & arms all of stone, & those splendid-necked, winged ones high in the air with strong lungs, built-in compasses, & clear reedy calls falling from sky to earth?

William Kurelek, *Inukshuk and Canada Geese* (1977).

31

Today the air teemed with status updates, though I had to listen very hard to hear them. Here's a handful of translations. Rock Dove: *In the bright light my neck was a rainbow curved until, collar-like, end touched end.* Crow: *Jabbed at a jack-o'-lantern—but the eyes were already pecked out.* Hemlock: *A few of my roots grew a millimetre more.* Red Squirrel: *Took a leap, ten leaps, thirty leaps—every day Leaping Day.*

NOVEMBER

...murmurations over the dark hills...

1

Two weeks after I first met her, the doe is back grazing along Wentworth Loop. Again she seems unafraid, unflustered, though she must hear my footsteps far better than I do. Maybe she's seen enough joggers, photographers & dog-walkers to be trusting. Her calm is flattering to my species, but I'm tempted to wave my arms & shout, "Beware, beware!" into the dark-bordered, upright ears.

2

Having just learned the Japanese phrase "forest swimming," I wind through the woods differently today. The air feels watery, the bracketed fungi on tree trunks is reminiscent of coral, & my breathing has a middle-of-the-river rhythm. The needling skeptic in me claims "forest swimming" is a hifalutin, roundabout way of saying "a walk in the woods," but the metaphor adjusts the atmosphere & refreshes my step.

> The standard translation of the phrase is "forest bathing," but I'm letting my mistake stand.

3

That spot falling through the dusk couldn't be windblown fur from a Weasel or a Snowshoe Hare, because both are still brown, weeks away from their winter white. Some gull's breast-feather tuft? An immaculate moth's torn-off wing? Autumn's first snowflake—concentrator of cold, forerunner of blizzards—throws across my memory many stories printed into winter fields with paws, claws & boots.

4

The switch from an hour of Standing Poses to a final fifteen minutes of Sitting Poses is like a return to earth, a plane's satisfying thud on a tarmac. How good to hear "Let every part of you relax to the ground." We've practiced Eagle & Crane & Warrior II, but now we're on our backs, in full contact with the mat—until we breathe into Bridge, arching upward, but with feet & shoulders pressed into terra firma.

5

"What do you think of when I say 'web'?" Overlapping voices answer, "The internet," "Google," "World Wide." Last summer, I tell the students, a spider with black & golden legs built out of itself a thready, symmetrical complexity by my back door. Silently I imagine their grandchildren saying, "Long ago, what a spider makes from its spit reminded us of the internet, so we started calling it a *web*."

6

Now that most reds, yellows & oranges have fallen & started down the long road to decay, it's time for Tamaracks to stand forth newly golden. Porcupines favour their inner bark & Ruffed Grouse their needles, while I honour their doubleness as conifers but not evergreens, & the way their spacey branches let light through. Not in June but in November I find these golden illuminations against a grey sky.

7

While days of rain drape the forest & seep into every rootlet & tendril, while deep puddles force you off familiar trails & coax you to find new ways of moving on, while the stream bursts its banks & crawls up over gone-to-seed cattails & submerges the footbridge, your basement back home stays dry, so out here you're spared the hand of panic, & gladness wells up within you for the rain's transforming extravagance.

8

The deluge has knocked free so many of the Norway Maple's leaves that our front lawn lies under a slick, slippery mass. The sidewalk, walkway & steps are also plastered with the yellows. A dozen Starlings stalk amidst the soddenness—out-of work but irrepressible vineyard workers stamping & trampling—catching between their claws the colours of butternut squash, lemon skins, old discoloured pages.

9

Three frogs croaked near a full cream-pail, its lid lying in the grass. As an old woman approached, the frogs went silent, jumped high, & landed in the creamer. They kicked, splashed, thrashed; two of them gave up & drowned. But the other frog paddled, turned & churned, the cream thickening & thickening. The woman watched the frog climb onto an island of fresh butter, then cheered as it hopped over her head.

> Adapted & condensed from *Will O' The Wisp: Folk Tales and Legends of New Brunswick*, by Carole Spray.

10

Yesterday on a naturalists' listserv: *Picked up an owl on hwy 14. Will freeze it. Any takers. Mel, Lake Echo.* By now that feathery carcass must be stiffened in a deep freeze, ice-blooded, neck-locked. Can anybody become the "taker" of an owl that is no more? Those former eyes—great gold & black drops—are blind, & the owl in all its completeness is long-flown, lost in a night from which it will never return.

11

At the Battle of Arras, Curtis Wills (1895-1984) caught a bullet in the back. If that wound hadn't forced him off the battlefield, he might've vanished later in the ferocity & carnage—& my mother, my five siblings, I & my two children wouldn't exist. So blessings on that wound, & blessings on any mud-trapped mule that—taking an earlier bullet, one headed for my grandfather's heart—kept the doorway to life open for us.

12

In a bookstore's parking lot the Royal Astronomical Society sets up three telescopes. She & I squint at Jupiter & a few of its many moons. We learn that Ganymede is crater-covered, Io volcano-pocked, & Europa ice-wrapped—& that Jupiter is fives times farther than us from the Sun, & a thousand Earths could fit into the ball of gasses that it is. But at this telescope I'm also looking through her breath condensed on the glass.

13

At dusk I walked home through streets where gangs have attacked six strangers in six weeks. Who knows what were the manifold, tangled reasons for the beatings? I resented the shadows' exaggerations, the back-of-my-neck tightness. Was I learning the fears of a rabbit smelling wolves, a hawk-unnerved mouse? I felt I was—though the "gangs" are made of young men & women with their own nightmares & names.

14

In the Empire Theatre my daughter & I gawk at owls battling owls—species vs. species—in deep-coloured animation. Their eyes widen with rage, their blood erupts like lava. Why do those birds, already beaked & taloned, swing sabres & wear gladitorial gear? A few rows away some guy keeps coughing, as if a pellet of bones & tiny skulls were about to pop from his gut.

15

For the first time in months the air goes sub-zero, making the most meagre ice on forest pools—though "ice" may not be the word for such feeble crystalization. If I were patient enough to spend hours waiting for the exact time when water becomes ice, wouldn't I still miss that fine-edged moment? A vole adrift, weighing under an ounce, would surely fragment such an infinitesimally thin raft.

16

Father Wolf taught him the meanings of things in the jungle, till every rustle in the grass, every breath of the night air, every note of the owls above his head, every scratch of a bat's claws, & every splash of every fish jumping, meant just as much to him as the work of his office means to a business man. But if every "every" were true, wouldn't Mowgli have fallen into madness long before reaching manhood?

Quotation from Kipling's *The Jungle Book.*

17

Last month the Blue Whale surfaced to take its place on the $10 stamp. Makes sense, as do the $8 Grizzly Bear & the $5 Moose. The niftiest surprises: 6¢ Assassin Bug, 8¢ Marginated Leatherwing, & 9¢ Dogbane Beetle. Then I see Canada Post labels those small ones "Beneficial Insects." So this question burrows & stings: will we ever invite onto our stamps the least conspicuous crawlers beautiful in their uselessness?

18

Nothing in these woods may be better named than Moosehair Lichen. "Are you sure that's not a bunch of moose's hair?" More ingenious: Methuselah's Beard Lichen. Though they didn't know about 900-year-old Methuselah until a minute ago, these children revel in saying that webby lichen's name. They tip their heads back to stare up at its long, long strands dangling from the higher branches in the middle of the swamp.

19

In a field outside Windsor, a black horse is lying on its back on bald earth, wagging its legs in the air, through which a scattering of near-invisible snow floats. Hard to believe how much the horse reminds us of our black kitten rubbing his spine into the floor. Such resemblances help keep chaos at bay. If we crossed the field, would we hear a purr of pleasure, the black horse waving its hooves at the clouds?

20

Cycling across campus where a Saw-whet Owl roosted four years ago, I see another—but no, it's a branch stub mimicking an owl, as the owl mimicked a branch stub. The bird of cinnamon, rufus & cream feathers never opened its eyes. *If sound sleep means a clean conscience, the Saw-whet has few sins on its head.* Four years too long without that unruffled visitor to the city, that small bundle of calm in the sky.

Italicized sentence from *The Birds of America*, 1936, general editor Gilbert Pearson.

21

TO CULL OR NOT TO CULL reads one pointed headline. No clear proof the slaughter of 140,000 Grey Seals would increase Cod stocks, but a reader responds, *Seals are never going to be extinct, they're like rats. You do-gooders want to save rats too? Man up to the issue, folks.* The phrase "man up" hits like the reek of something rotting on shore—but "cull" cuts, sharp tool of a verb, a blade seeking a simple solution: cull, cull, cull—

22

In a wire cage a Peacock shrieks & honks. While his feathers' highlights are blue, green & golden, his voice is red. In the wild he would make the same cries, but how can we not hear protest or pleading? To our startled ears each cry is the Peacock's way of keeping a grip on his uncaged self, the self that—though the feathers keep their lustre—diminishes, goes hungry, & withdraws into straw interwoven with shadow.

23

Among millions, this forest-floor segment, 1' x 1': Sphaghum Moss the lime of Sea Lettuce—spruce cone ridged with sap like dried grey glue—semi-circle of Pixie Cups, tiny red parasols—wishingbone-shaped twig—beige feather in dark water a circumference of 6 inches. At a glance the forest looks uniform, but you could wander for acres & weeks & not find another segment like this—or that—or that—

24

Rereading Basho's haiku about cherry petals falling into soup & fish salad, I recall a picnic when maple samaras spun down into potato salad & fruit punch—& the day my brother, overjoyed by our lost cat's return, tore a petunia from the garden & ate it. That had nothing to do with hunger, everything with humorous, earlyteen impulse, as if Andrew could celebrate only by imbibing bright colour, becoming part blossom.

25

The inescapable reds of November. Crabapples fallen onto asphalt, blood-coloured gems of broken necklaces. Burning Bushes bordering a neighbour's lawn—their cold fires. While the maple leaves murmur *crimson, vermillion* & let their leaves go, Karen drives to Value Village with her old coat in a bag, about to give someone else the chance to be as bright as a singing Cardinal.

26

For days the skies have let down torrents of rain. The fire logs have sung upon my hearth, and I have been happy in the instincts that flower beneath a roof. The sky is still heavy with unshed drops, but the human frame would stand no more confinement. I walked in the woods with boot & stick, hunting that fresh surface of experience, that touch & smell of reality without which a philosophy soon becomes metaphysics.

Slightly condensed from November 26th entry in *An Almanac for Moderns* (1935), by Donald Culross Peattie.

27

Do we need the piano & the trumpets? On the computer screen, murmurations of starlings spread over the wide sky, thousands & thousands, synchronized gatherings wheeling, climbing, sinking, the common stubby bird that downs French fries or gags on greasy paper now part of an aerial wonder. Bam bam—the bass drum kicks in. The music bullies our ears. Aren't the murmurations over the dark hills & the blue water enough?

28

Time to sing your praises, Caddisflies. You secrete silk for your larval cases & fortify them with pebbles & twigs. You're moth-like but haunt streams & lakes. You fold four hairy wings over yourself like tents. You are an order, not a species. Your antennae are often longer than your body. You purify, eating debris of the living. Even in November you enliven the night & the moonlight. Trout & salmon feast on you.

29

The silent pad of the great cat, hardly turning a stone; the cunning hoof of the deer, adapting at every step—feet for all surfaces, all necessities of weight & speed. Walking is a series of falls & recoveries, so insensibly merged there is no saying where the fall ends & the recovery begins. In walking we are playing with gravity. The instant we lose our poise our step becomes a stumble, & we the sport of gravity.

A collage of sentences from two essays, "The Beauty of the Foot" and "The Art of Walking," by Bliss Carman, in *The Making of Personality* (1908).

30

The old National Dream, leading to the Last Spike, has detoured into another dream: Rails to Trails, coast to coast. By Governor's Lake, a cyclist's jingling bell is the distant cousin of a CPR blast. Yet the setting sun is the giant light of a train coming our way, the past still present—like the ghost of some bewildered conductor wandering the woods, searching for the lost train & the elusive rails.

DECEMBER

...things we take on faith...

1

In bare-branched December, what was hidden is revealed: warblers' nests, no longer sheltered, now fraying & empty. But nobody is around to say which fledglings hardly breathed after cracking out of the egg, which ended up in hawks' bellies, & which are now fully-feathered & firm-muscled—already thousands of miles distant, with only the thinnest bonds left to those abandoned nurseries open to the winds.

2

Along Five Island Lake most leaves fell earthward while still moist & flexible, but the brittle, curling oak leaves stay on their twigs. They're well on their way to decay even before blending with the decomposition at our feet. Though lacking red or orange, they reassure us with their stubborn reluctance to let go, their holding earthly browns against the sky as the cold hours lengthen & frost attacks their stems.

3

The vegetarian buys meat for his family. At a check-out, chicken legs & stewing beef in plastic send guilt ripples up his arms. For decades he was an omnivore, so he's not about to say, "You eat it, you buy it." At home he hears distant bacon frying. A barge of good memories floats his way—oh maple-flavoured mnemonic aroma! His son teases, "Smell that, smell that?" The vegetarian has never known a pig or a lamb by name.

4

At the Field Naturalists monthly meeting, where we've heard talks about sharks, warblers, volcanoes & orchids, tonight's guest delves into his years of diving in Halifax Harbour. His eyes are lit up with a collection of artifacts: old bottles for ginger beer & Minard's Linament, International Colonial Railway padlocks, a rare, slim-stemmed clay pipe. For field naturalists, a peculiar hour: a mirror giving us stories only of our own kind.

5

In Seaforth an albino Red Squirrel, white as a weasel in winter, scrambles along branches. No, it didn't fall into a bucket of ivory paint: all that whiteness, rising from the fur-roots, looks true, alive as any red. That creature doesn't strut like a rule-breaker—it's all squirrel, all eagerness & balance. Late afternoon, we drive home westward, facing a sky stained a rust-red we take a minute to recognize.

6

The Bear & Orion, the Pleides, great things beyond understanding, without number. But ask the animals & they will teach you: sulphur is scattered, the teeth of the young lions are broken. "The light," they say, "is near the darkness." Iron as straw, bronze as rotten wood. The east wind claps its hands & hisses. Can papyrus grow where there is no marsh? Caravans turn aside from their course, go up into the waste.

A collage composed of bits extracted from nine chapters in the Book of Job (Revised Standard Version).

7

Walking to work I hear high-pitched winds around my iPod's ear-phones, competing with Fred Eaglesmith live/solo. Fred's stories are as long as his tunes: he jokes, "a gazillion songs about relation-ships." The winds' music is minimalist—but it changes pitch now & then, veering away from total monotone. If our ears were keen enough, Fred, we might think winds have a gazillion variations on the theme "empty & driven."

8

Ten years ago during the weeks of a nervous breakdown, I took long baths & read the labels on bottles of body oils & shampoos. Foam arose from extracts of Ginger, Lime & Lavender, my hair coated in Aloe Vera Leaf, Oak Tree Bark, Jojoba Seed, Horsetail & Marigold. I laughed to discover that Prusus Serotina (Wild Cherry) did its bit to calm my haywire serotonin. Those lists on the labels were like waterfalls of balm.

9

Healthier, in the bathtub I now read more than the labels on shampoo bottles. Charles Wright's *Sestets*, for one. "Walking Beside the Diversion Ditch Lake." "Autumn Thoughts on the East Fork." "Description's The Art of Something or Other." "Terrestrial Music." Yes, "empty & driven," yet tonight in cooling water I'm mulling over a table of contents, drawn into nothing but the beauty of titles.

10

A fruit fly in my ear: "What's there to eat"? From his basement den Ursus stomps upstairs, sniffing for meat or berries. My son is thirteen & hungry. A sparrow digs about in a cupboard, eager for bread & peanut butter. A crow flutters in a huff & opens the fridge door with its beak. Growing longer limbs, Josh is hungry morning, afternoon & night. "What's there to eat?" The jaws of the fourteenth year stretch wide.

11

Last night the children finished their study unit on water by staging their play simply called *The Drought*. The ending—greedy hyenas learn to share a newly discovered well—was buoyant. Yet now I recall most sharply a trio of grade ones wrapped in striped cloaks, wandering on & off stage, chanting raggedly, "Thirsty, thirsty—we are thirsty zebras!" in small dry human voices.

12

In the past week our kitten Hitch has smashed a wine glass, poked holes in drapes, lapped our soup, & chewed book dustjackets. Whiskers aquiver, he climbs up to the pot of flaming-red poinsettia, noses the stems aside, & plays with the soil. Confined, work-heavy, deadline-tied, I miss the forests & rocky plateaus & shores. After scolding & shooing Hitch, I stoop & roll between my fingers bits of earth scattered over the floor.

13

How little it takes for beauty to emerge. Early winter, water is still open where the shade isn't so constant & thick, but here in the ravine's depths a frozen stream: opaque ice etched with ovals, diagonals, curves, crosses. Not a lesson in geometry, not a window onto anything otherwordly. Just unique ice, blue & milk-white, its patterns configured by many undetectable makers.

14

Seized by wet winds along the coast, three Dovekies plummet into a field miles inland. Imagine us, landlubbers, stranded, thrashing in salty waves. Those thick-necked, blunt-billed birds weaken since banquets of plankton & copepods aren't everywhere. Here's their hardest, last lesson: the wind that keeps them from flying back to the sea may be the only reminder of home left as their feathers fluff under the blast.

15

Bedraggled & alone, a Killdeer lingers on Crystal Crescent Beach, stepping through grass bared by patches of melted snow. By now it should be either sheltered inland in this province, or warmed by sunlight thousands of miles south, not found among these shells, rocks & ice-fingers—yet the unpredictable is predictable, say the disjointed cliffs & the forever-breaking waves along this brutal coast.

16

Sibilant, slipping down the sky, only a dozen Cedar Waxwings defy the quiet of the snowy coastal trail. You might think the sounds of this cold clarity should be bells—a ringing, a chiming, something of brass or glass—but the twelve-voiced slurring is welcome. Then the waxwings go silent, & fidget in a leafless tree. Did their voices stop because their blood whispered warnings of freezing, perilous rain?

17

Any season is birchbark season, but with some colours now vanished & frost whitening the bent dead flowers, fewer things pull our attention away from those bands encircling the birches, alternating grey & beige & ivory. One loose pink strip hanging at right angles to the bands—Moccasin Flower pink—stirs in us the question whether, in early winter, any shade of summer has gone utterly into retreat.

18

A Mallard & Black Duck hybrid pair paddle among a pond's glassily clear reflections. Any watcher might be disoriented by those two drifting over dark branches & through cumulous clouds & across the sky's quivering blue. The mirrored world on the water is upside-down & second-hand, but what do the ducks care?—the element they trust holds them up & yields to their orange feet.

19

A homebound, birdless day reduced to that ancient pair, rain & wind. Cloudwaters tap on the eaves & the chimneytop—a xylophonist unable to break his trance. Then air-rushes smother the drumming, let loose their roofbuffets, their bricksighs & wallcreakers. Chimney-fixated, drinking Darjeeling, Assam, Russian Caravan, I try to fathom living in a world full of sounds but no voices.

20

In the Maritime Museum of the Atlantic, the Kraken draws us in with its legendary diet—whales, ships, humans. The ceiling-tall model flings its many arms out & up. In 1735, says a guide dressed in yellow rubber, Linnaeus welcomed the octopus-crab-leviathan into his *Systema Naturae*, only to withdraw it from later versions. "That's even worse than going extinct," says a schoolboy. He clarifies, "Never to have been!"

21

Can you pull him in with a fish hook, or tie down his tongue with a rope? Iron he treats like straw, bronze like rotten wood. Who can penetrate his double coat of armour, or open the doors of his face? Will you make a pet of him like a bird, or put him on a leash for the young women of your house? Will traders barter for him? He leaves a glistening wake behind him; you would think the deep had white hair.

Adapted from the Book of Job, chapter 41, mostly the Revised Standard Version, with some influence from the New International Version.

22

At Red Bridge Pond, hope to see the reported Common Gallinule—uncommon in these parts. Scan for the sedge-favouring one—no luck. Ready to declare failure, turn away—then the dark, paddle-footed bird launches onto the pond. A minute ago, I thought I'd be writing about absence. Now the afternoon offers the gift of presence, the Gallinule unmistakable, reddish back feathers revealed in the bright cold light.

23

In today's newspaper one article is like a gap in a snowbank, through which I slide into Wolverine territory. That rarely seen climber crushes bones too tough for Grizzlies or Cougars. *1000 pounds of attitude*, says a biologist, *in a 30-pound body*. Its metabolic rate would stagger & collapse us. I'm filled with satisfaction that the Wolverine exists, though I have scant chance of ever coming across even a hair from its coat.

24

Closer than the container ships & tugboats & dories, Kelp Flies swarm over the kelp mounds, their bristly bodies & legs restless as the waves. Those predators the sandpipers have gone south. In sub-zero air, the insects draw warmth from the overlapping, frost-touched strands, their diet narrowed to decaying seaweeds. Through all four seasons Kelp Flies are utterly at home here, finding everything they need in the wrack zone.

25

Laura is so keen on her present to me it's the first I open: a sock monkey, turquoise & black, complete with ears & tail. "I thought," she explains simply, "you'd write a poem about it." Earlier this month an ancient bone in a Siberian cave gave the first DNA to ID unknown contemporaries of Neanderthals. My daughter eagerly hands me a shining, intangible gift: being imagined as Father Who Writes Poem About Sock Monkey.

26

Saint Stephen's Day is Boxing Day is Hunting the Wren Day. They say the Wren let Vikings know where the Irish were by beating its wings on their shields. So Celtic communities caught the birds, killed them, & tied them to a staff decked with ribbons & flowers—then paraded around, pleading for money. Thus does a story construe & pinpoint a villain. Even a small bird, a winter singer, is strangled to satisfy a desire for sacrifice.

27

In flight from merciless law, a woman & a man slept in a cave with their child & their donkey. Hubbub of horses: a metal-plated soldier held up a lantern. But across the cave's mouth a spider had quickly built a giant web, all tensile symmetry. The strangers—saying "not one strand broken"—sped away. Then only the child woke up, but he didn't make a sound while gazing at the dawn-lit web from within the darkness.

28

We go uphill as easily as downhill. Platero pricks up his ears, dilates his nostrils in his upraised hair until they almost reach his eyes, & exposes his large yellow teeth. He is breathing in from the four winds some deep, indefinable essence. Yes. There, on another hill, fine & gray against the blue sky, is his beloved, & double brayings, long & sonorous, break with their clamour the luminous hour, then fall like twin waterfalls.

Condensed passage from *Platero and I* by Juan Ramón Jiménez, translated by Eloïse Roach from the Spanish.

29

Just enough snow for a barely white Noël, then rainfalls give us brown & yellow days. Sinking boot-heels aren't surprising, but I've never before walked past so many maples densely spotted with green foliose lichens, up the trunks' heights & along the branches' lengths—those rampant patches the colour of a sea's pale green shallows. On this cloud-pressed morning they're the shredded, widely flung signature of the saturated air.

30

At the ravine's foot where the thin stream is frozen, Golden-crowned Kinglets & Black-capped Chickadees, with two Downy Woodpeckers, cavort non-stop in a small spruce. They don't "ornament" the branches—they're living, restless & vocal, all *tsees* & *dees* & *kiks*. The season & appetite have brought them together. I sweep snow off a boulder & sit to watch the varied patterns & good sense of a mixed flock.

31

No action around the beaver lodge by Frog Pond, but the mud-locked branches' tips look fresh & sharp. If the water freezes, the great-incisored ones will spend more hours underwater, or in the chambers they engineered. Beneath the surface their feed-piles are stored, feasts for months. Without diving to inspect, we take that on faith. On our walk the things we take on faith outnumber the twigs overhead & underfoot.

JANUARY

...release into the atavistic...

1

My daughter's quick eye catches an otter running across the thin ice of Frog Pond. Last night watching a DVD of *Guys & Dolls* we asked how many mink died for the wraps hugging the dancers lined up in front of gamblers & gangsters. We slip through the woods until we reach shore & find those eyes & whiskers much closer to us & the mud. As I whisper, "New Year's Day of the Otter," the lustrous mammal disappears under the ice.

2

These are dog-walkers' woods—or, more exactly, woods of walkers & dogs. With the deciduous sound-buffer now grounded, in the distance two dogs bark repeatedly because of an alien scent, a challenging stare, or a territorial urge. Then again, they could be barking for joy, in their shared, all-too-brief release into the atavistic. Or is that just the mood of this dogless walker who was at his desk an hour ago?

3

In a grey-blue sky late today, only three scraps of clouds near the horizon—like dark shirts unclaimed on a battlefield after the troops left, all the dead & the wounded carted away. So the sky is a place where a crucial thing occurred, & winds have scribbled out all signs of the event but for those smoke-like patches, those three dark shirts, those ambiguous, stranded exceptions to the blue.

4

On a great root at the lake's edge I rested. The old spruce jutted horizontally out over the water, then curved upward. No branches grew from the bank side; all reaching was toward the lake. Peculiar spruce in a precarious place. When I resumed my walk, I felt lopsided &—a pinched nerve? watching that tree for so long?—favoured my right leg, as if all the branches of my thought & senses were now on that side.

5

After a light snowfall I looked under a wide-reaching spruce & saw a perfect circle of orange-flecked green around the trunk. Had that tree's roots melted the snow on the surrounding grass, moss & needles? Then I realized, the branches—the branches kept all snow from under there. But for hours afterward I valued my short-lived mistake, that dream of generous roots heating the earth under the spruce.

6

Cursed with worn wires, the ancestral home caught fire, then was razed & sent to oblivion, while the last remaining cousin left for the West. The mill had already collapsed into its stream. Under historic rainfalls the pond now overflows, rips & stunts the dam. Fire & water have done their work to subtract my family from the land; earth & air are also around to help rust, blow down, & bury every sign of us.

7

The only species that thinks it needs zippers keeps on making ones that don't work. In The Bay I fight with three jackets' catches, then settle on big-buttoned zipperlessness, pleased with that solution. I silently laugh to find a label calling the inner material FAUX FUR. When I buy the falsehood-lined jacket & wear it home, the otter & the seal swim into my mind, & I envy them the warmth they make out of themselves.

8

Early morning walk to the cornerstore—caught, glad to be caught, between two unseen Black-capped Chickadees calling from opposite sides of the street. They whistle *feebee feebee* as if to each other—or are they isolated, outside dialogue? No branch knocks, no car stutters. Ground is rock-hard, sky grim white. I'm tempted to say those two-note whistles defy the sub-zero air, then suspect they're beyond defiance, closer to cheer.

9

One of my students gives me a story about dragons—his prose exact & free of hokey names, fire-breathing & dialogue. What leads a twenty-year-old to write such limpid sentences about dragons? Even his battle scenes are restrained. (Quietest student in the class.) Maybe he's closely watched wide-winged birds swooping outside his window, & a pet iguana's neck pulsing as he feeds it turnip greens & mango.

10

Long tails of mice have whipped up the snow. This is the one season when we see their crisscrossed dashes' windings & off-the-cuff loops. Snow speaks of them as grass, moss & leaves don't. As Mac said on *C.S.I. New York*, "Best investigative tool money can't buy—snow." But no crime has occurred here, not even where a trail ends abruptly in the middle of a field, with a faint red splotch in the disrupted white.

11

Half our dining-room table is occupied by an in-progress jigsaw-puzzle of *The Peaceable Kingdom*. What drove the Quaker Edward Hicks (1780-1849) to paint sixty canvasses of wolf & lamb, leopard & kid, bear & child lying down together? Do we truly want to complete that puzzle overturning the order of so much we know? All teeth are hidden, the paint of the pale sky is cracked.

12

Last year on Sullivan's Pond, the Coots—cherry-red eyes, slate-grey plumage close to black—harassed streaky brown Gadwalls. But now a Gadwall is going after a Coot's breakfast. What would you do if a neighbour blustered into your house & helped himself to your toast & eggs? Table-turning morning: the restoration of balance looks comical as Gadwall challenges Coot for the same dripping bunch of grasses & roots.

13

So pleased to bring this abundance home!—then in our Nova Scotian kitchen the labels say the strawberries are from Florida; the raspberries, California; the blueberries, Chile; & the blackberries, Mexico. I toss them together for our waffles & fetch the bottle reading PURE NOVA SCOTIAN MAPLE SYRUP—WESTCHESTER NS. Like locavores' thickened tears, the syrup flows down the hills of berries.

14

Where Rhodora bushes bloomed six months ago, a light snow-cover over the narrow trail, fresh prints of a previous walker & a dog. On summer days I didn't know when anyone had last walked that way. A little snow makes such a difference: clear reminder I'm following the footsteps of others. So I wander farther to find printless snow, to indulge in the pride of feeling like the day's trailblazer on a well-worn trail.

15

In Pets Unlimited, a Scarlet Macaw steps sideways, back & forth, along a brief perch. A Cocker Spaniel presses its nose against mesh. By jars of Siamese Fighting Fish, two children argue. "That one's dead." "No it's not dead." "Yuh—floating means you're dead." "That other one's lying on the bottom, but it looks dead." "Maybe they're both dead." "This shouldn't be called Pets Unlimited if they're dead."

16

This is a province that calls for a scope on a tripod: on winter beaches the distant becomes near, the indistinct clear. Those smudgy ducks amidst rocking grey waves? White-winged Scoters, white commas around their eyes. That isolato even farther out? One Common Goldeneye, a larger white patch on its face. When binoculars are too weak, the scope is a superior eye, like a poem magnifying the amorphous, the unreachable.

17

Along Eastern Passage we focused our binoculars on Ring-billed Gulls, a Wigeon with her sky-blue beak, an agitated, doomed Killdeer. Then in the distance, in thickening, whipping snow, hawk-favoured Devil's Island vanished. On the slow drive home my memory returned less to the watched birds than to those snow-hidden, great-winged ones singling out mice & rats uncamouflaged on the island's white reaches.

18

This is a Yoga pose I didn't know: Dying Bug. Okay, flipped on our backs, we lift & shake our arms & legs. "Dying but not dead," Maxine clarifies. "You're still alive in your core & limbs." What would Kafka say? Surely he wouldn't let Dying Bug morph into Eagle or Sun Salutation. Outdoors it's too cold for pupae to split open: snow pellets the size of short-grain rice tick against the windows.

19

Over breakfast & newspapers, Karen says, "Listen to this! 'The Giant Amazon Water Lily has leaves 7' wide. It blooms at night, white & female at first. Its strong scent lures beetles. The next night, now male & bright pink, it releases the trapped, pollen-coated insects. Then they fly to another white lily, where the pollen rubs off on the female.'"All this taught & learned so early, the morning tea still hot!

20

I was called out to see E's cave in the snow. The walls were one universal reflector with countless facets. When E crawled into the extremity & shouted, it sounded ridiculously faint. At first I could not believe he spoke loud, but we all of us crawled in by turns, & I saw that we might lie in the hole screaming for assistance in vain while travelers were passing twenty feet distant. The snow drank up the sound.

Condensed passage from the January 20th 1857 entry in Thoreau's journals.

21

On the edge of a forest I walked past a knife shop. Sunlight struck the blades in the windows. Like no such shop in crime-familiar streets, that one seemed cut loose from brutality, as if its knives could only trim branches for a shelter or a splint, or carve an animal shape into a tree stump. But I remind myself how a knife carried into a forest might also spear a fish in a brook, or open an angry bear's throat.

22

In the forest around Six Mile Lake I search for tracks besides my own, but the only marks in the snow are punctures of water drops fallen from branches. A friend once gave me 350-million-year-old rain-splash signatures on rock. But with more snow or a melting, these marks won't last. The percenage of drops fossilized through the ages must be so small I can't imagine how many zeros would go after the decimal point.

23

A congregation of Cattails surrounded by snow, locked in by ice, their rhizomes hidden in muck. Under the name Cossack's Asparagus they sound more edible. Before they split open in spring in slow motion, these seed-heads survive cold months, packed tight with a quarter of a million seeds—more concentrated, I imagine, than anything else in sight but for the brain & wits of a Crow flying low over the marsh.

24

Last year, 208 "new species" were found in the Mekong River region. Pompadour-bedecked, snub-nosed monkey. Wolf Snake, fangs in both its jaws. Limestone Leaf-warbler, its voice loud out of all proportion to its size. A Pitcher Plant mighty enough to devour rats & small birds. When we say "new species," how short is our sight? Couldn't their ancestors date back to millennia before our earliest roots & branches?

25

At the edge of the falls, dispersed twigs & nuts & leaves are like sealed specimens, but the dominant ice also contains other ice: blue marbles, yellow lozenges, green globes, & finger-length silver trees. Among root & rock, a length of curves & ripples: a fetal shape on an ultra-sound screen, but three-dimensional under the ice. On my knees, I can believe birth is at home even here where the cold waters flow & fall.

26

On the snowmobile-scarred trail to Five Island Lake, stapled paper signs said a collie named Summer was lost—hit-&-run victim, shy four-year-old, photographed in a florid garden. "Summer!" called a bass voice from beyond a coniferous wall. "Summer, Summer, we're here!"—soprano from a roadside. A week later, a strip of masking-tape over each sign says FOUND! yet the snow is deeper & the air colder.

27

A Day Without God, says a wayside pulpit, *Is Like An Unsharpened Pencil. It Has No Point.* Brothers & sisters of Faith Tabernacle, I beg to differ. If "points" are neither messages nor morals but vivid spots of time, then the air & the trees are full of them. Some days the world is a fine acupuncturist, & anything—Red Crossbill's spruce-cracking, Brown Creeper's vanishing—leaps from nerve to nerve, sharpening the walker's alertness.

28

A quartet of minor milestones today. A stretch of fresh pond ice more imprinted with Mallard & Wigeon feet than any I'd ever seen. A new personal record for closeness to an Iceland Gull (it rested on kelp as if exhausted or sick, then, effortlessly, up & away). The first Yellow-breasted Chat ever to enter my vision, feathers of startling radiance, then one birder saying to another, "Thanks for the Chat," the spontaneous pun a struck bell.

29

Half the birds we saw yesterday exposed the narrowness of our naming. Red-necked Grebe, Rough-legged Hawk, Long-tailed Duck—as if our human neighbours were Spotty Face, Donkey Laugh, Carrot Hair, Big Prick. Such names were like the distant Canada Geese in the yellowed grasses—nothing of goosekind visible but for their heads & necks, as if their upper selves were adrift, the rest forgotten or lost.

30

Five Baltimore Orioles nudge clusters of purple grapes in a neighbour's backyard. "Oriole cage" misses the mark, because they aren't trapped but easily enter, eat in & exit from the wire structure. At home I recall Betty Carter jazzily singing "Baltimore Oriole" & wonder who pitched for the Orioles in 1965. But this afternoon a few blocks away, I watched the orange quintet pierce grapes flown northward thousands of miles & suspended over snow.

31

Teeth of plant-gorging Sauropods are extracted from the earth 150 million years after the beasts breathed their last. Oxygen in the enamel, experts say, differ from the surrounding sediment's—a clue that the long-necked ones wandered hundreds of miles, hunting for leaves & stems & stalks, from floodplains to highlands. Teeth & bone. Matter, matter—the stories it tells us, if we bend & listen hard enough.

FEBRUARY

...red blood, black bird, white snow...

1

A midwinter night at Neptune Theatre, school kids tackle *A Midsummer Night's Dream*—the heart of it all not a duke or lover but quickfooted Puck, who tricked a bean-fed horse by neighing, & hung out as a crab in a gossip's bowl. Tonight in Halifax, what could he turn into? A wind tugging off every toque on Argyle Street—a harbour rat raiding Pizza Corner—a gull protesting in the face of the Clock Tower.

2

Until last winter I walked home in the dark after Monday evening classes, through raw cold or bulby snow or forehead-numbing rain. Twenty years of that, but now these nights I have the car & fly home in comfort—so why this nostalgia for the old walks, the flesh-&-blood ritual? Laughable, I suppose, laughable—as if the next step were to torch the car, flee to the woods, throw away my razor, & catch fish bare-handed!

3

A mild morning, the windows open at breakfast, the redbreasts singing. Walked with Coleridge over the hills. The sea at first obscured by vapour; that vapour afterwards slid in one mighty mass along the sea-shore. I never saw such a union of earth, sky, & sea. The clouds beneath our feet spread themselves to the water, & the clouds of the sky almost joined them. Gathered sticks in the wood; a perfect stillness.

Condensed from Dorothy Wordsworth's *Journals*, February 3, 1798.

4

Bare plant-stalks stiff as wicks & long as human arms poke from the open water at one end of the frozen lake. Many times melted & solidified, whitened by its entrapped snow, ice encircles each stalk like candle wax. If you waded out with a torch & lit those skinny arms, those wicks, night skiers in the distance might briefly mistake them for fish leaping up from the lake & turning into arrows of fire & light.

5

One falling snowflake melts on the tip of a tongue, but many millions together are something else—what a lake is, say, to a drop of water it holds. A through-the-night blizzard has closed down all schools. On our walk home from a greasy-spoon lunch, Laura climbs the plow-heightened banks. Slides, kicks, thrashes. Her laughter-filled falls & recoveries celebrate the arrival of this new continent in our midst.

6

Beyond a red barn roofed in black, in a field all snow, a crow digs its beak into something raw & bloody. Red blood, black bird, white snow: pastels & pastorals seem no more, lost in elementals—then I lift my eyes an inch higher & find at the field's end a line of dark green & another of pale blue, & above them billows of white cloud, background for three flying crows—more black hungry for red.

7

Phalanxes of tripods & giant lenses line the roads around Sheffield Mills. Eagle Watch Weekend: the great birds descend from blue heights & grab freshly dead chickens scattered across the snow like breadcrumbs for sparrows. In exchange, they let us featherless, pancake-stuffed bipeds watch & record. A mile farther on, I'm refreshed to find a lone eagle deep in a thick spruce, only its head & neck visible.

8

In deep winter, food dwindled & hunger grew. A father followed snowshoe tracks to a lake, where an old man in a wigwam gave him a gift of moose meat. Back home, he opened the pack & found nothing but poplar bark. Had his host been a beaver? Dreaming of great rodents roasted, villagers raced to the lake, but oh dizzying, double deception: no sign of lodge or wigwam, beast or man, marked the lakeside snow.

A retelling & radical condensation of a Mi'kmaq tale told to & adapted by Silas Rand in *Legends of the Micmacs*.

9

Granite boulders & a granite plateau lead to a middle-of-the-woods surprise: a spruce-surrounded lake. All that rock predates human footprints & petroglyphs. Ferns drained of their green are already the colour & dryness of fern fossils. A Raven rending the silence over the lake may sound just like its primeval ancestors. Nothing coaxes me to think of the watch on my wrist or the wallet in my pocket.

10

...form large flocks in winter, say the guidebooks, but this morning we only find one Horned Lark—low flyer, shuffling walker. It flicks forth in a blast of fine wind-blown snow, then edges, halting, up a plunging ridge. White drifts have climbed over & closed many coastal bushes, yet the larks don't retreat to sheltering woods. Once an open-ground bird, always an open-ground bird: small, loyal, storm-harassed.

11

From MacCormack's Beach we watch a Red Fox trot along the shore of Lawlor Island. No foxes breed there, so we guess he wandered to the mainland's edge onto an ice-block before it became an ice-floe. He turns & retraces his steps among the shells, sand, mud & rocks. Nothing guarantees another ice-floe will give him return passage. Luck & wits aren't enough; that fox may be exploring the limits of his final home.

12

Over the lake a stranger on snowshoes has left a near-perfect oval the length of a hockey rink. Is that trail the lake's one statement, the rest of its whiteness silent & blank? If someone swam the same route in summer, the wake would instantly blur into invisibility. Winter gives us a chance to know where the stranger went, that oval the shape of an enormous snowshoe.

13

Right wing, left wing, teams named after birds. "He's flying," we say, "flying down the ice"—but however quick & graceful, he's grounded, gliding, his skates cutting the ice in the paradox of earthly flight. No aerial flute melody rises over our heads & raised arms; now & then a bullhorn bellows, more mournful than celebratory, like a trapped elephant calling from a muck hole, an elephant wanting wings.

14

Manhattan

O streets of pretzel stands, neon signs higher than houses, & wide-striding text-messengers. On Fifth Avenue, citizens brush & bump me in single-minded rushes, triggering signals of claustrophobia in my chest. I think Robots first, then reconsider: they're caribou in a herd, fish in a school, & I'm the peculiar one, wanting to trace a protective space around me, denying my hoofed or finned community.

15

In Chinatown, on a PEKING DUCK HOUSE banner, a duck wearing a chef's hat, as if ducks roasted ducks. In the Museum of the Moving Image, a mechanical Hollywood wolf propped up, its metal innards exposed. In MoMA, the luscious orange of Franz Marc's *The World Cow* (1913). Near Times Square, a carriage horse I thought was called MAXIMUM RAT, until I stepped to one side & saw the whole sign: MAXIMUM RATE.

16

In the vast terminal of the Staten Island ferry, a pair of glittery-necked pigeons crowd into a drinking-fountain. They flutter up when a laughing boy approaches, then swoop back to quench their thirst. Over ten minutes I see them interrupted again & again by human drinkers. Skittish, yes, but persistent, rubbing their beaks against the metal basin to sip the dregs of municipal water they claim as theirs too.

17

At the Met, Arcimboldo's *The Four Seasons* (1587): a human-shaped head made of wizened matter, blunt stubs of snapped-off stalks, grapes & apples & cherries, & bare branches like antlers. We love fruit to pluck, but what happens when it sprouts from our flesh like cankers, & the boundaries between us & what we grow dissolve? Where are we then? As I gaze at the uncanny head, goose-bumps multiply on the back of my neck.

18

I jotted down little things just as they occurred to me, for though they might appear trifling today, they might add up tomorrow to form a picture of the planet's voyage. I noted down thousands of details: black water filled with icy needles tinkling as it washed against icebound islets, gulls mistaking floating ice for fish, the night the lake grew silent with telephone wires alone humming over the dead valley.

Abridged from a passage in *Nature's Diary* by Mikhail Prishvin (1925), translated by L. Navrosov from the Russian.

19

Back in Halifax

This winter's snow is erratic but there's no mistaking the season for summer, when I have full faith in the ground & hardly need glance at it for minutes. Today along Rockingham Trail, in low, shadowy stretches, sedimentary-like layers of ice are slippery & risky. Though gentler than a rollercoaster's, the dips & rises demand attention. Curve the trail through a metaphor: it's less indulgent & tougher-minded than during easy summer.

20

The rare Common Gallinule is still at Red Bridge Pond. When cold & ice expand their rule, a "rescue party" of six arrive with hip-waders, nets & a kayak, but the reed-lurker proves elusive. *Too much fuss over one bird,* says some on-line skeptic, *look at the big picture.* A man spreading chopped greens, fishcakes, & canned salmon shares a childhood tale of Hummingbird helping dowse a forest fire one beakful of water at a time.

21

In the Farmers' Market, Laura chose a clear-beaded necklace for a friend's birthday. Now while she's in dance class, I find small globes on the twigs of leafless birches & willows. Out of this very day the raindrop-necklace link is created anew. I paid the necklace's maker, but nobody needs payment here among the expanding puddles, & the beads will break & vanish if you try to carry them away.

22

Is nothing perfect? Along Sailors Memorial Way the light seemed incomparable for watching a pair of Red-breasted Mergansers near shore—their crests more than ever like wild, wind-blown hairstyles, their eyes & long serrated bills redder than anything else in sight. They swam at the same slow rate, as if pulled by one string. Had I ever seen anything more clearly? I'm *saying* the late-afternoon light was perfect.

23

Once again the snow has withdrawn from our lawns & streets & retreated to become grainy vestiges in shadowy alleyways. Wavering winter—pingpong weather—fickle February. But at Black Rock Beach I find stretches of the pocked & ribbed rock coated thinly in ice like frozen milk. That much cold is still with us. You never need look far to find something opaque. Here at my feet, the spilled milk of winter.

24

Weaving gait, hyperactive, hearing loss: JITTERY 2. Smaller, reduced open-field activity, develops late-onset tremors upon movement: SMALL LETHARGIC. Male and female hypogonadism: WEE WILLIE. Lethargic, weak limbs: DEPRESSION 2. Polydactyl hind feet, shortened, widened long bones, splayed gait: CHARLIE CHAPLIN. Seizures, followed by rapid tail movement: RATTLE. Head tossing/circling in both directions: HEADTOSSER 8.

> All words & phrases from "Wee, Sleekit, Cowrin," *Harper's,* May 2004: "From descriptions of genetically modified mice ... [in] the Baylor College of Medicine's Mouse Mutagenesis Center for Developmental Defects."

25

Nine years after the record-setting winds swiped & struck, the hurricane's wood sculptures remain. While thousands of broken trees were sawn & trucked away, others still stand, long-dead, stripped of all bark, bone-grey, bone-white, bone-cream. Their trunks, smooth as any woodcarver's work; their branches, arms caught in ambiguous gestures. From devastation their stark, elegant symmetries & asymmetries were built.

26

Half a century ago, when "bird" began to separate in my awareness into many species, Evening Grosbeaks mobbed across winter roads. So many dozen paraded—like sheep reincarnated as birds—that my father drove slowly, to keep from crushing them. Their population peaked, & now those yellow & black garlands of tropical brightness thrown over northern roads scramble for seeds of memory, between snowbanks of memory.

27

All things do go a courting, in earth or sea or air. Cousin J. has made an Aeolian harp which plays beautifully whenever there is a breeze. Our pastor says we are a "worm." Let us strive together to part with time more reluctantly, watch the pinions of the fleeing moment until they are dim in the distance. I hear robins a great way off, & wagons a great way off, & rivers, & all appear to be hurrying somewhere undisclosed to me.

A collage of sentences, some condensed, from five of Emily Dickinson's letters written between 1850 & 1874.

28

My one time in Brazil, I wandered into a sand-surrounded Copacabana shop & bought a beach towel imprinted with a family of jaguars. Over the next decade we took that towel to parks & beaches, then after Hoodoo was diagnosed with a brain tumour & injected, we wrapped him in the jaguars & buried him by our garden. I hoped it was no toothed irony but an atavistic gift, swaddling so domestic a beast in ones so free-roaming & lithe.

29

For leap years

Long ago a review swatted me for writing a line about a "prepositional trail" winding through the woods—but I still hold onto that phrase. Today along St. Laurent Trail the frozen day felt full of between, by, into, across, around & through. The sentence "A squirrel up a tree jeers at me" shrank into "A squirrel a tree jeers me"—then filled up again. With each footstep: above & beyond, before & after, over & out.

MARCH

...whatever the singer has weathered...

1

Pale green Usnea lichen rests on snow like a tuft of beard on a barber's floor. Did wind, sliding ice, or a woodpecker's claw knock it from its tree? Nearby, over a black boulder Xanthoria lichens form deep orange patchwork, afixed so fast that no winds or claws peel them off. I pick up the Usnea & rest it on the Xanthoria, the tenacious & rockbound now a companion to what floats free & falls.

2

Have you made an herbarium yet? My business is circumference. The birds father rescued are trifling in his trees—how flippant are the saved! The kitchen wall is covered with chilly flies trying to warm themselves. I want to write so much I omit digestion. Friday I tasted life—it was a vast morsel. We go to sleep with the peach in our hands & wake with the stone, but the stone is the pledge of summers to come.

A collage of sentences, some condensed, from seven of Emily Dickinson's letters, written between 1845 & 1875.

3

Sunglasses lost, I squint hard against overwhelming brightness. Except for coniferous green, wherever I look new snow has laid its claim on boulders, branches, fence posts & the edges of streams. I'm about to call the snow a dictatorship when I see violet spots, aquamarine spots, leaping against the trees, a trick for light-stunned eyes: prisms built & broken, intense insubstantial colours blinking against the white.

4

Leafing through a Musical Heritage Society catalogue, tempted by so much. Time to get other versions of Haydn's "The Creation," Debussy's "La mer," or Dvořák's "Silent Woods"? To hear Dreller sing "Three Ravens" & walk along Janáček's "On an Overgrown Path, Books I & II"? Can I resist a recording by the Audubon Quartet? Surely, surely I should know Ives's "Universe Symphony" (unfinished at his death).

5

Run-off has risen high over the wettest part of the trail to Two Mile Lake, so I turn back & compensate for the cut-short trek by returning more slowly. Going more slowly means extra minutes with the map-sized patches of Sphagnum Moss: soaked, lime green, profuse. No colours in the world of Jaguars & Howler Monkeys surpass in brightness this green of a northern forest floor in late winter.

6

Desultory drumming: binoculars bring a Black-backed Woodpecker into focus—his barred flanks & yellow crown. Once called Arctic Three-toed Woodpecker, that species favours the north: I can't say of other woodpeckers, "I'm in the south of its range." Bark-flaker, grub-finder, he reminds me north & south aren't absolutes, & the coloured bands on range maps—narrow or wide, purple or pink or blue—mirror feather patterns.

7

For the first time in half a year, before my eyes open I wake to a Song Sparrow's scintillations. *Melospiza melodia*. In this province some Song Sparrows hang around all winter, others migrate to warm, green groves. Can the pace & intonations tell anyone if the bird is freshly back, or not? No answer arrives. But that singing is an opening to buds, blossoms & nest-building, whatever the singer has weathered.

8

In a lumber camp a century ago, a sullen woodsman took pride in his crop of curly black hair. His hatred of Whiskey-jacks grew when they picked bread & moose meat off his plate, so he trapped one & plucked every feather from its back & chest. When the naked Whiskey-jack died, other woodsmen said, "You'll be some sorry." In the morning, when the jay-killer looked in the mirror, his head was as bare as a peeled log.

Adapted & condensed from *Will O' The Wisp: Folk Tales and Legends of New Brunswick*, by Carole Spray.

9

Back to Red Bridge Pond for the uncommon Gallinule, this time with Don visiting from Newfoundland. It chugged along with bobbing-head momentum, climbed onto bunched, flattened reeds, & splayed a webless, claw-like foot. Later Don thanked me twice—but the bird-givers were the winds, the sea surges, this unpredictable winter, & the happenstance of a pond appearing when the disoriented bird needed shelter.

10

Fiddling with Sci-Tech Expo program before awards ceremony, I silently gave prizes to kids' project titles. For headiest title: STIMULATE YOUR BRAIN. Most market-awareness: FAST-FOOD DECAY. Greatest playfulness: DOES DOODLING HELP STUDENTS LEARN? Title with most impact for parents past their forties: DOES FEAR CHANGE WITH AGE? Most buoyancy: LIFE-SPAN OF A BUBBLE.

11

The door of your patio's wooden gate bangs. Blustery, bright. That door, its rusty latch off-centre, bangs. In the kitchen, you don't want to put on boots. Winds rising, that door bangs. Won't some nerve-rattled neighbour rush outside to adjust the latch? Bang. Some days you wish the air indoors were without walls, open to all that circulating. But your patience takes a beating as the door bangs, bangs.

12

A TV screen in this greasy spoon displays quake-sunken & tsunami-flattened neighbourhoods in Japan. Then the floor shakes—vibrations from a transport truck?—& the waitress says, "It's the Judo students upstairs—starting early today." The class shakes the walls, but not as the earth buckles & uprises & overcomes our will. The Judo students are minor movers, so we walk home along a straight, still sidewalk.

13

Gliese 581g—a "new planet" (could be older than ours)—orbits in a Goldilocks zone, neither too near nor too far from its star. But with 20 trillion miles to travel, a space ship from Earth would need generations to reach it. So don't volunteer, my unborn grandchildren: keep me from imagining your grandchildren living all their years encased in glass, plastic & steel, never knowing mud, sand or rock under their feet.

14

Sheree sends a photo of her hand shadowed on a blank sheet of paper—a rabbit's head clutching a pen. Shadow puppets leap against my memory—dark on pale walls, the heads of horses, dogs, & goats, wide-winged birds in flight. Such devisings of light & shadow, & games like Leap Frog, Duck Duck Goose, & Monkey in the Middle, inspire an edging-into-transformation hunch: some days to be human isn't enough.

15

Today in Yoga class I chose a spot by the windows. Often when a sideways turn or twist was to the right, I couldn't resist glancing out at the first blue sky in a week, cirrus clouds stretched like gauze. Later during Crane, cumulus drifts chugged along, a thickened substantiality. Then when I rose from the utter calm of Shavasana, the sky was noon-lit, cloudless, but too full of blue to be a tabula rasa.

16

Our two-trunked Silver Birch is far shorter than the old Sycamore & Beech keeping the sunlight from it. Year after year a third of its leaves are brown & hole-riddled, yet we can't bear to saw it down, & we value the shade that sickens it. This birch is an overprotected child—the friendless son touching the hearts of guests who recognize in themselves his air of quiet, the shadows of his fears, & his explicit ribs.

17

Last week the Tohoku earthquake, they say, tilted the earth's axis "infinitesimally yet measurably." On the other side of the world, resting on rocks by small meltwater-swollen falls, we watch leaves & twigs caught in the flow. Neither the chickadees flicking nearby nor our inarticulate grief can change the planet's axis, even infinitesimally. More twigs & leaves are propelled helplessly into the onrushing stream.

18

Alerted by my walk's vibrations, a Razor Clam starts its quick smooth digging & disappearing. *Ensis directus* (straight arrow) lifts like a drawbridge toward perpendicularity, its foot-anchor sinking farther until nothing but sand remains. What deft burrowing! I imagine Razor Clams live a few months, but when I get home & read that they reach twenty years, their longevity says, *Anything on earth should live this long.*

19

Took our fly rod & done some paddling, Paul e-mails the listserv. *Fish both native & invasive not interested, so I'm cooking store trout for supper. Smells good though. Beavers were 100 m out & carrying stuff—would swim a long piece before the house was finished. They had stripped the bark from the base of a red maple & the sap was running—it had gathered so many flies the chewed-off area was black. Beavers helping flies!*

20

The earliest Painted Turtle I've ever seen, sunlight probing its corners & grooves, its carapace a dark green close to black. Did it stay on the jutting rock & let me get close to its leathery eyelids because it was so fresh from hibernation, immersed in the rediscovery of radiant mid-day warmth? A nearby dog snarled as if eager to flip the reptile over, so I lingered, admiring details close-up—the head's yellow stripes, the neck's red stripes.

21

Spring's calendar-sanctioned first day has come & gone, garden beds & lawns bared for half a month—but this morning outside the window, a slight layer of snow. If we had the leisure, we could sit around all day arguing whether winter has lumbered from its cave for a final night, shedding its extraneous whiteness, or whether spring, more rascally than its reputation says, is scoffing at the year's unfolding.

22

For four miles to the granite summit, the ten of us vowed to stay silent & spin a few lines. Gwen bent to her notebook so often she later said, "I was on fire." To Nate I mimed amusement at my cluster of post-it notes vs. his buckram-bound 200 pages. Though his blank book weighed more than my notes, it was good to see. *If you walked slowly enough,* I heard it say, *all my pages would be filled up, like razed land turned into forest.*

23

On the granite barrens we hear a fluster of duck voices, from an unseen pond or pool hidden in the evergreen density below. They're disembodied, without lungs or beaks or clear location, yet they sound full of spring, the old spring before weather was twisted askew. With those hearty outbursts, how easy it is to imagine the breaking & transporting of cold-killed reeds that support warm new life.

24

No flowers bloom yet on the trail, but shaggy birches—loose bark-strips breeze-jiggled—look ready to shed. From crown to ground, a Black Spruce's pale inner wood is exposed, a long sheared-off strip fallen onto mosses & mud, thanks to a lightning bolt's clean, quick work. The roots of an old Red Spruce grip a giant boulder under it: who can say how & why it's grown there, lasting against all odds, probing earth & sun?

25

Name the forest like a pub, & today it isn't The Crown & Thistle or The Fox & Hound, but The Crow & Chickadee. In such quiet, sound is distilled to two species: the chickadees slur rather than call, & the crows' notes—neither owl-on-the-premises shrieks nor father-crow-is-dead keenings—sink fast. Dry-throated, I sit on a stump, drinking to its dregs a bottle of water, surrounded by empty stone chairs in The Lazy Wanderer.

26

You drive across the steel monolith spanning the harbour, past Irving oil towers & mega Ultramar refiners & hundreds of fresh-off-the-container-ship cars wrapped in white like mummy cloth, along a narrower road until you stop your car, cross beachstones, & bend to barnacles smaller than your pinkie's nail, those crustaceans as stubbornly adhesive as their stubborn ancestors aeons ago.

27

Through the Economies (Lower, Middle, Upper) the mud at low tide is muted red, despite the downpour. A brighter shade of red is on alert in the crest of a Pileated Woodpecker flying past the windshield. Doomsayers, the radio reminds me, insist today is Judgement Day. But how can the fiery lava of mere predictions compare with that big woodpecker's flame, or those mud flats so thick & far-reaching in the rain & the mist?

28

On the Wolfville mudflats terns cry *kiri-kiri-kiri*, a quick overlapping of thin voices thrown into the wind. We swivel & scan, scan & swivel, but don't see the long-winged white birds—can't even be sure if they're to the left or right, in front or back of us. Avian ventriloquists? But then the excitement's gone. You say a dozen, I say three or four—overstatement & understatement returning hand-in-hand to Front Street.

29

Out of the brightness broke coals of fire. Up from the desolate pit, out of the miry bog, set my feet upon a rock. Springs gush forth in the valleys, give drink to every beast. The high mountains are for the wild goats; the rocks are a refuge for the badger. My heart flows with a goodly theme, though the earth change. I am gone like a shadow at evening. I am shaken off like a locust.

A collage from six chapters in the Psalms (Revised Standard Version), with fragments often condensed.

30

In Thailand & Malaysia, meticulous Swiftlets build nests from their saliva. The sticky wetness dries & hardens. Meanwhile the illegal trade in bird's-nest soup is up to half a billion dollars a year, & men on bamboo ropes strip cave walls bare. Those nests provide no taste or nutrition, yet tradition is in the saddle and whips us on. Didn't the Swiftlet give us enough, merely in being one who makes crystalline cradles from its own spit?

31

Sunlight falls liberally upon the storm-shattered shells scattered over shore. You might think some fierce-wheeled machine had lumbered back & forth, fragmenting everything brittle—whether blue, pink or creamy white—but tumults of winds & waves & rocks did the work. The air is an ocean of winks. The beach is so aglitter, so much like a dumping ground for broken mirrors, you have to look away.

SOURCES

Ammons, A. R. *Worldly Hopes*. New York: Norton, 1982.

Carman, Bliss. *The Making of Personality*. Boston: L. C. Page, 1908.

Chekhov, Anton. *The Letters of Anton Pavlovitch Tchehov to Olga Leonardovna Knipper*. Trans. Constance Garnett. New York: George H. Doran, n.d.

Clare, John. *John Clare*. Ed. Eric Robinson and David Powell. Oxford: Oxford University Press, 1984.

Crawford, Mattie Rose, William Scott, John Dearness, and Will Elliott. *Public School Nature-Study*. Toronto: Copp-Clark, 1902.

Dickinson, Emily. *Letters of Emily Dickinson*. 1894. Ed. Mabel Loomis Todd. Mineloa, NY: Dover, 2003.

Emerson, Ralph Waldo. *Selected Journals 1820-1842*. Ed. Lawrence Rosenwald. New York: Library of America, 2010.

Geffroy, Gustave. "Claude Monet Exhibition." *Monet: A Retrospective*. Ed. Charles F. Stuckey. New York: Beaux Arts Editions, 1985.

Hass, Robert, ed. & trans. *The Essential Haiku: Versions of Bashō, Buson, and Issa*. New York: Ecco, 1994.

Hopkins, Gerard Manley. *Gerard Manley Hopkins*. Ed. Catherine Phillips. Oxford: Oxford University Press, 1986.

Howe, Joseph. *Western and Eastern Rambles: Travel Sketches of Nova Scotia*. Toronto: University of Toronto Press, 1973.

Jiménez, Juan Ramón. *Platero and I*. Trans. Eloïse Roach. Austin: University of Texas Press, 1957.

Kipling, Rudyard. *The Jungle Book*. Oxford: Oxford University Press, 1987.

Kurelek, William. *Kurelek Country: The Art of William Kurelek*. Toronto: Key Porter, 1999.

Pearson, T. Gilbert, editor-in-chief. *Birds of America*. 1917. Garden City, NY: Garden City Books, 1936.

Peattie, Donald Culross Peattie. *An Almanac for Moderns*. 1935. Boston: David R. Godine, 1970.

Poteet, Lewis. *The South Shore Phrase Book*, rev. ed. Halifax: Nimbus, 1998.

Prishvin, Mikhail. *Nature's Diary*. 1958. Trans. L. Navrosov. New York: Penguin, 1987.

Rand, Silas Tertius. *Legends of the Micmacs*. New York: Longmans, Green, 1894.

Roethke, Theodore. *Straw for the Fire: From the Notebooks of Theodore Roethke 1943-63*. Ed. David Wagoner. 1972. Seattle: University of Washington Press, 1980.

Slocum, Joshua. *Sailing Alone Around the World*. 1900. New York: Dover, 1956.

Spray, Carole. *Will-o'-the-Wisp: Folk Tales and Legends of New Brunswick*. Fredericton: Brunswick Press, 1979.

Thoreau, Henry David Thoreau. *Journal Volume 3: 1848-1851*. Eds. Robert Sattelmeyer, Marle B. Paterson, William Rossi. Princeton: Princeton University Press, 1990.

—. *Journal Volume 4: 1851-1852*. Eds. Leonard N. Neufeldt, Nancy Craig Simmons. Princeton: Princeton University Press, 1992.

—. *Journal Volume 5: 1852-1853*. Ed. Patrick F. O'Connell. Princeton: Princeton University Press, 1997.

von Bingen, Hildegard. *Physica: The Complete English Translation of Her Classic Work on Health and Healing*. Trans. Priscilla Throop. Rochester, VT: Healing Arts Press, 1998.

Waddell, Helen, trans. *Beasts and Saints*. London: Constable, 1934.

"Wee, Sleekit, Cowrin." *Harper's* May 2004.

Whitehead, Ruth Holmes. *Stories from the Six Worlds: Micmac Legends*. Halifax: Nimbus, 1988.

Wordsworth, Dorothy. *Journals of Dorothy Wordsworth*. 2nd ed. Ed. Mary Moorman. London: Oxford University Press, 1971.

Wright, Charles. *Sestets*. New York: Farrar, Straus and Giroux, 2009.

ACKNOWLEDGMENTS

For publishing sections of this book of days, sometimes in earlier versions, gratitude to the editors of the following: *Germination, The Goose, The Malahat Review, The New Quarterly, The Telegraph-Journal*.

Selections from the calendar were read & discussed by the author at the ALECC (Association for Literature, Environment & Culture in Canada) Conference in Sydney, NS, August 2010; the 9th U.N.B. Poetry Weekend in Fredericton, NB, October 2010; the Green Words / Green Words Conference in Toronto, ON, October 2011; 100 Mile Verses: ALECC Regional Reading Series in Wolfville, NS, March 2012; the Canadian Creative Writers & Creative Writing Programs Conference in Toronto, ON, May 2012; and the ASLE (Association for the Study of Literature and Environment) Conference in Lawrence, Kansas, May 2013.

Special thanks to Nancy Bauer, for weaving so many of these pieces into her "Salon" column in the Saturday *Telegraph-Journal*; Allan Cooper, for his belief in the prose poem & his great enthusiasm; Kim Jernigan, for welcoming nearly 50 of these prose pieces into *The New Quarterly*; & Cate Sandilands, for inviting me to the Green Words / Green Worlds Conference to give a "keynote address" about this book when it was still a work-in-progress. A revision of that address, transformed into an essay discussing the origins & development of this book, appears as "'Bitter-sweet-sweet, bitter-sweet-sweet': The Poetics & Politics of Writing A Nature Calendar," in a forthcoming anthology from Wilfred Laurier University Press, *Green Words / Green Worlds: Environmental Literatures and Politics*, edited by Catriona Sandilands and Ella Soper.

Other thanks for sustained, strong, or special support for this book to Pamela Banting, Gerry Beirne, David Boles, Robert Boschman, Louise Fox Burley, Akou Connell, Adam Dickinson, Jeffery Donaldson, Dale Estey, Tessa Chaffey Ftorek, Paul Huebener, Colleen Kitz-Goguen, Travis Lane, Chris Lister, Jean Malinson, Don McKay, Terry Pulliam, Jamie Reid, Elena Aquilar Saiz, Brenda Schmidt, Sandy Shreve, Ella Soper, Merna Summers, Lisa Szabo-Jones, Yvonne Trainer, & Susan Zimmerman. Much gratitude to Anne Compton & Robyn Sarah for recommending the manuscript one day over lunch with Evan Jones, & to Evan, falcon-eyed editor extraordinaire.

Love to Karen, Josh & Laura, my closest companions on this planet.

ABOUT THE AUTHOR

Brian Bartlett is the author of seven full-length collections of poetry, including *The Watchmaker's Table*, *The Afterlife of Trees*, and *Wanting the Day: Selected Poems* (Goose Lane Editions/Peterloo Poets UK). His books have received the Atlantic Poetry Prize and the Acorn-Plantos Award for People's Poetry. He has also been honoured with two *Malahat Review* Long Poem Prizes and first prize in the Petra Kenney poetry awards. Bartlett has edited volumes of selected poems by Don Domanski, James Reaney, and Robert Gibbs. He grew up in New Brunswick, lived in Montreal for fifteen years, and since 1990 has taught creative writing and literature at Saint Mary's University in Halifax.